social media, social justice, and the political economy of online networks

social media,
social justice
and the
political economy
of online networks

social media, social justice, and the political economy of online networks

Jeffrey Layne Blevins
and James Jaehoon Lee

University of
CINCINNATI | PRESS

About the University of Cincinnati Press

The University of Cincinnati Press is committed to publishing rigorous, peer-reviewed, leading scholarship accessibly to stimulate dialog among the academy, public intellectuals and lay practitioners. The Press endeavors to erase disciplinary boundaries in order to cast fresh light on common problems in our global community. Building on the university's long-standing tradition of social responsibility to the citizens of Cincinnati, the state of Ohio, and the world, the Press publishes books on topics that expose and resolve disparities at every level of society and have local, national and global impact.

The University of Cincinnati Press, Cincinnati 45221
Copyright © 2022

This book is freely available in an open access edition thanks to TOME (Toward an Open Monograph Ecosystem)—a collaboration of the Association of American Universities, the Association of University Presses, and the Association of Research Libraries. Learn more at the TOME website, available at: openmonographs.org. Requests regarding this work should be sent to University of Cincinnati Press, Langsam Library, 2911 Woodside Drive, Cincinnati, Ohio 45221 ucincinnatipress.uc.edu

Published in 2022

ISBN (paperback) 978-1-947602-84-7
ISBN (online resource) 978-1-947602-86-1
ISBN (ePUB) 978-1-947602-85-4

Names: Blevins, Jeffrey Layne, author. | Lee, James Jaehoon, author.
Title: Social media, social justice, and the political economy of online
    networks / Jeffrey Layne Blevins and James Jaehoon Lee.
Description: Cincinnati, Ohio : University of Cincinnati Press, [2022] |
    Includes bibliographical references and index.
Identifiers: LCCN 2021050468 | ISBN 9781947602847 (Paperback) | ISBN
    9781947602854 (ePub) | ISBN 9781947602861 (PDF)
Subjects: LCSH: Communication in politics. | Social media--Political
    aspects. | Social justice--Public opinion.
Classification: LCC JA85 .B54 2022 | DDC 320.01/4--dc23/eng/20211210
LC record available at https://lccn.loc.gov/2021050468

An enhanced open-access edition of this book is available at:
https://ucincinnatipress.manifoldapp.org/projects/political-discourse-on-social-media

Designed and produced for UC Press by Jennifer Flint
Typeset in Maiola Regular
Printed in the United States of America
First Printing

contents

social media,
social justice,
and the
political economy
of online networks

social media,
social justice
and the
political economy
of online networks

chapter 1

social media and our political and economic lives

The Capitol riot in Washington, D.C. on January 6, 2021 was an infamously historic moment for the United States, as it was only the second time in the life of the nation that its statehouse had been breached. The first time was on August 24, 1814, when British adversaries set the Capitol building on fire during the War of 1812, when Congress was in recess. In January of 2021, though, it was some of the country's own that stormed the Capitol while Congress was in session to certify the results of a presidential election, and many of the insurrectionists posted images and livestreamed video of the violence on their social media accounts as it unfolded.

Not only did social media play a role in documenting the events of January 6, 2021, it was arguably the primary platform for unfounded claims of election fraud and calls to action that precipitated the rioters' march into the Capitol. Then-president Donald Trump, a lame duck incumbent who lost his re-election bid to Democratic rival Joseph Biden, had refused to concede his defeat. On his Twitter account he steadily promoted baseless claims of election fraud and promoted a rally that would ultimately precipitate the mayhem, tweeting on December 19, 2020: "big protest in DC on January 6th" adding "Be there, will be wild."[1] The U.S. House of Representatives impeached Trump for incitement of the insurrection that day, and his Twitter messages before, during, and after the Capitol riot were used as evidence against him during the impeachment trial. Throughout the day on January 6, Trump tweeted inflammatory messages, including two that were flagged by Twitter and later deleted, before the social media company permanently suspended his account two days later.

The Capitol riot and the permanent suspension of a U.S. president from Twitter were, perhaps, a strange coda to the story that had been unfolding about the role that social media had played in the Breonna Taylor and George Floyd protests during the summer of 2020 and the social justice activities taking shape on social media since Ferguson in 2014. How did social media, which evolved through message boards, personal spaces on the web, and connecting with high school friends on Facebook, become so integral to our social, political, and economic lives? Why are digital platforms designed for recreation so useful to both the causes of social justice and right-wing authoritarianism? What does the front line of popular politics look like on social media?

Our initial approach to these questions was to combine political economic analysis and explore social media networks to further our understanding of social movements and political action. Simply put, "political economy" is the study of power and money. Derived from eighteenth-century Enlightenment thinking, it is based in moral philosophy and examines the interrelationship of resource allocation, production, distribution, laws, and government within societies. Of course, "political economy" should not be confused with the scholarship under the title of "economics," which branched off from the political economic tradition in the nineteenth century and focused more on micro-economic analyses (without the moral philosophy). Despite the popularity of pure "economic" research, scholarship under the banner of "political economy" has remained in several other forms, including the "political economy of media." As described by Dallas Smythe, Vincent Mosco, Janet Wasko, Eileen Meehan, Robert McChesney, Peter Golding, and Graham Murdock, as well as several others, political economy of this variety examines ownership and control of media institutions; relationships of power among media industries, regulators, audiences, and advertisers; as well as laws and policies that impact media behavior and content. The political economy of media is morally oriented, and its methods of inquiry are often multidisciplinary, drawing from historical and legal analysis as well as critical and social scientific approaches.

Our approach in this book was to blend political economy of this variety with social network analysis, which broadly aims to understand how groups of people engage, coalesce, and clash over issues on social media. We focused primarily on the Twitter platform and how users tweet, tag others, like and share other users' posts, and use hashtags. How does Twitter activity grow organically and how can it be manipulated? How do tweets go viral? And more significantly, what kinds of social, cultural, and political narratives emerge through social media networks? What does a "social movement" (conventionally defined in terms of strikes, protest marches, or sit-ins) look like through visualizations of these networks on social media? And how might these visualizations of movements taking place on Twitter reshape our understanding of how political action takes place in the digital era? We aim here to contribute to a more comprehensive understanding of how social media may empower and hinder social justice activity.

We explored these questions through a series of data-based case studies of Twitter activity, including tweets during the Ferguson demonstrations in 2014 when the hashtag #BLM trended, the 2016 presidential election season when Donald Trump's #MAGA hashtag came into prominence, and throughout the summer of 2020, when nationwide protests occurred around the #BlackLivesMatter movement and another presidential campaign season. While the goals of social justice advocates and political groups may be different, we are curious about how they might intersect on Twitter, especially as social justice is often linked to popular politics. The examination presented here relies on both data analytics and qualitative analysis, as we provide political economic context for the most used and impactful hashtags in the immediate aftermath of Ferguson, as well as describing how hashtags went viral during the 2016 election season and throughout the summer of 2020. We also address the meanings and implications of these activities and hashtags. Our work here is decidedly large-scale in method and yet critically determined, as we consider the scope of social justice activity on social media and examine it within the broader context of the political economy of misinformation, disinformation, and so-called fake news.

One of the key features of our work is the use of machine learning methodologies to develop a unique and engaging look at social movements on social media. We examined large data sets of tweets, retweets, comments, and hashtags to parse the semantic discourse within Twitter archives, and then digitized all of this data to create rich images and 3D modeling of the Twitter networks during distinct periods of time during social and political movements as they took shape over the past several years. Our analysis also engages critical political economic theory and network analysis to create an interactive look at the role of social media activity such as Twitter posts in social justice and political campaigns. We explore this feature and describe our methodologies in more detail in the open-access version of this book from 2021 (available at https://ucincinnatipress.manifoldapp.org/projects/political-discourse-on-social-media), as it was specifically designed for peer data researchers and other experts. However, the 2022 print version that you are reading here includes more narrative about what all of this research means for how we as a society understand the role of social media in social justice movements, popular politics, and the economy, as well as our own personal lives.

Before we examine social justice and political activities on Twitter in the current age of fake news and post-truth, as well as network manipulation by bots, the influence of commercial interests, troll farms, and clever memes that shape public discourse, we must first return to our original question: How did social media, which evolved through message boards, personal spaces on the web, and connecting with high school friends on Facebook, become so integral to our social, political, and economic lives?

The rise of social media platforms

Social media platforms are a byproduct of internet development, which began in the 1960s and culminated in an early internet prototype created by the U.S. Department of Defense and university researchers, known as the Advanced Research Projects Agency Network (ARPANET) in 1969.[2] A commercial version of ARPANET called Telnet was created in 1974, and the first "major development toward social media sites" came about in 1978 with an online bulletin board system in Chicago, which included announcements, meetings, and other information posted by users.[3] With the growth of home computing systems and modems in the 1980s, internet service providers (ISPs) such as Prodigy in 1984 created relay chats and news sharing for their users, while America Online (AOL) featured member profiles that were organized into communities.[4] With the development of the World Wide Web, ISPs such as Mosaic, Prodigy, and AOL began offering their users access to the World Wide Web in the early 1990s, and their popularity grew in a matter of years. In 1993 there were just over 200 web servers online, just over 1,500 in 1994, and over a million by 1997.[5] While there was no website specifically referred to as "social media" in the mid-1990s, the concept of social media has existed at least since the mid-1990s, as there were many sites that featured elements of today's social media. For instance, several websites allowed users to post comments, later referred to as "web logs" or "blogs." AOL's instant messenger "chat rooms" were popularized in the 1998 film *You've Got Mail*, starring Tom Hanks and Meg Ryan. Other websites created in the mid-to late 1990s, such as Classmates, SixDegrees, BlackPlanet, AsianAvenue, and MiGente allowed users to create personal profiles, create groups, and identify friends—all of which are features of what is commonly known now as "social media."

Danah Boyd and Nicole Ellison defined social media as "web-based services that allow individuals to (1) construct a public or semi-public profile within a bounded system, (2) articulate a list of other users with whom they share a connection, and (3) view and traverse their list of connections and those made by others within the system."[6] In the early 2000s, other social media sites, such as Friendster and MySpace, came along, but it was not until Facebook was made public in 2006 that social media grew even further in popularity and developed more permanent features, such as the "like" button, which has been adapted on other social media platforms and apps. Also in 2006, another social media mainstay, Twitter, was developed and allowed its users to "follow" each other. Additionally, Twitter featured cross-platform connectivity, so that users could more easily share other online content to and from Twitter, as well as their other social media channels. Twitter is an open network in which people can "follow" other accounts, while Facebook is established on a more closed "friend" structure. Both Facebook and Twitter now provide instant communication (including images and videos) to large numbers of friends/followers, while also affording one-to-one communication, similar to AOL's early instant messenger service. YouTube also emerged in the mid-2000s, as a platform specifically for sharing user-generated video content. Users have their own "channels" and can post comments on videos posted by other users. YouTube and Facebook, along with Twitter and now others, also feature cross-platform connectivity, which was an important element for users to quickly disperse content across an array of online-based media channels during the Arab Spring in 2011 and Ferguson in 2014.

The development of smartphones and tablets, such as the iPad in 2010, have made social media more accessible and popular. Today, social media applications are most often used with mobile telecommunication devices with either iOS or Android operating systems, allowing users to post images and livestream videos from their mobile phone's camera. These critical features were employed by protesters, journalists, and other social media users during the Breonna Taylor and George Floyd protests throughout the summer of 2020.

Social media and hate groups

Hate groups have also employed early internet services, such as online bulletin board systems and newsgroups, and later, social media platforms, to create, find, and facilitate like-minded networks. In fact, hate groups were organized online well before those interested in social justice.[7] While the specific counts varied, by 2001 there were somewhere between 800 and 2,200 hate group websites, newsgroups, clubs, and other types of communities organized online.[8] One of the more recent networks of racist, white nationalist, and other hate-based groups used Facebook to organize the infamous "Unite the Right" rally in Charlottes-ville, Virginia.[9]

The Southern Poverty Law Center (SPLC) defined a hate group as an organization that through "official statements or principles . . . or its activities" has "beliefs or practices that attack or malign an entire class of people, typically for their immutable characteristics."[10] Hate groups denigrate and attempt to inflame public opinion against certain groups of people based on skin color, race, religion, ethnic origin, age, gender, or sexual orientation. The targets of hate groups are often blamed for an array of social, economic, or political ills. Internet-based platforms, including social media, have provided a useful form of networking, organization, and communication for these groups, as they are easy to access, inexpensive, and provide anonymity if necessary. Online and social media can also be used to bring in revenue through merchandising and donations. More critically, it is difficult for the government to inter-dict the activities of hate groups online due in part to Section 230 of the Communications Decency Act of 1996, which provides broad immunity to interactive computer service operators, such as social media outlets, for content posted on their services by third-party users.

Furthermore, blanket statements of hatred toward ethnic, racial, reli-gious, or other groups are protected in the U.S. by the First Amendment to its Constitution. Only threats and intimidation (which may be based on racial, ethnic, gender, or other animus) directed at specific individu-als are not protected by the First Amendment. Therefore, the regulation of hate speech online is at the discretion of internet service providers, social media outlets, and individual websites. Some of these interactive service operators prohibit hate speech or certain groups through their "terms of service" statements. For instance, Facebook removed several pages used by racist and white nationalist groups from its service after the fatal "Unite the Right" rally in 2017. YouTube banned Atomwaffen's channel in 2018 after the group praised the killing of Blaze Bernstein, a gay Jewish college student. Atomwaffen's videos had featured armed group members yelling slogans about killing Jews. And in 2021, Twitter suspended more than 70,000 accounts linked to the Capitol riot, including then-president Trump and other users linked to the QAnon conspiracy theory movement.[11] This minimal form of industry self-regulation is the only kind of limitation for hate groups networking online and through social media.

With limited government interdiction and minimal industry self-regulation, social media networks have been useful platforms for hate groups to organize, such as the "Unite the Right" rally, or spread harmful conspiracy theories. For instance, David Duke, a former Grand Wizard of the Ku Klux Klan and key figure in the "Unite the Right" rally in Charlottesville, sometimes tweeted 30 times a day to nearly 50,000 followers.[12] Moreover, social media outlets, including mainstream platforms Twitter and Facebook, have been used to spread QAnon-based conspiracy theories.[13] QAnon is an unknown source of an unproven far-right conspiracy theory that insists that a group of Hollywood elites and Democratic politicians are engaged in pedophilia, child sex-trafficking, and Satan worship, among other outrageous claims. While QAnon originated on a 4chan message board, its theories are spread by users on more popular social media outlets.[14]

The social media landscape leading up to Ferguson

Social media have become a dominant force in many of our social, political, and economic lives. By 2013 Facebook and YouTube had more than one billion users worldwide, while Twitter boasted more than 500 million, with the average American between the ages of 18 and 64 spending an average of over three hours per day on social media.[15] Social media have become a significant source of interpersonal connection with friends and family, information gathering and sharing, political organizing, and job networking on sites such as LinkedIn. No matter whether one sees this level of consumption and engagement with social platforms as good or bad, we can at least agree that it has pervasive presence in our lives and that sheer presence alone demands critical attention. Beyond connecting and sharing for entertainment, diversion, and escape, social media use has become a way that we acquire all sorts of social, cultural, and political knowledge, including social movements on both the left (e.g., Black Lives Matter, Ferguson, George Floyd, etc.) and the right (MAGA, Unite the Right, Stop the Steal, etc.).

With social media, essentially anyone can be a storyteller. Social media and mobile streaming applications have demonstrated that the relationship between news media and the public is subject to change in significant ways, as virtually everyone now has the potential to document and livestream events to a global audience. To say the least, social media have become a primary venue for public commentary about current events, disrupting the gatekeeping power once held by national news outlets.

While we survey analyses of all social platforms, we concentrate our analysis on Twitter in the chapters that follow. Twitter was not only the social medium of choice for Donald Trump and the historic event that took place on January 6, 2021, but it has been the primary social medium for engagement between professional and citizen journalists covering social justice movements[16] and is the most "normalized" social medium for journalistic activity.[17]

Accordingly, our analysis will begin by examining how social media empower and influence social justice movements, focusing on Black Lives Matter and Twitter. We will also take a look at how social media platforms affected social discourse about social justice during Ferguson in 2014 and a year later in Cincinnati, when @BlackLivesCincy had a role in the aftermath of the Sam DuBose shooting. From there we analyze conversations taking place on Twitter to understand how networks of discourse affect social and political movements, including an analysis of the tweets during the U.S. presidential election cycle of 2016, when Trump's signature hashtag (#MAGA) emerged. Finally, we consider how misinformation and disinformation on Twitter complicate analyses of social media and social justice movements. Amid social justice groups working from the bottom up and political forces pushing from the top down, there are also commercial interests generating unnatural networks and connections between people, creating the complex political-economic struggle taking place over online networks that is the subject of this book.

Cincinnati covered the @BlackLivesMatterCincy group that mobilized after the shooting, and provide a critical examination of access to internet, mobile media, and legacy news among low-income groups that shapes social justice efforts in significant ways. Through further political economic analysis, we examine the need for social justice activists to support media policy reform in the aftermath of the killing of George Floyd by Minneapolis police officer Derek Chauvin on May 25, 2020. Chauvin, who is white, pressed his knee into the neck of Floyd, who was Black, as he lay prone in the street with his hands cuffed behind his back. Floyd was unarmed and apprehended for suspicion of using a counterfeit $20 dollar bill at a convenience store. As onlookers recorded video of Floyd as he pleaded that he could not breathe, video that would be shared on social media in the weeks that followed, they also appealed to Chauvin and the other police officers that looked on to stop or intervene before Floyd became unresponsive and died. Videos of Floyd's death were shared on social media and television news outlets, as people gathered by the thousands in cities across the U.S. and world to decry police violence against Black people. Throughout this period the hashtag #BlackLivesMatter trended on Twitter and other social media outlets.

With #BlackLivesMatter as an emblem, social media and Twitter in particular has become the frontline for social justice advocacy and debates following the deaths of unarmed Black people at the hands of police or neighborhood watchdogs, beginning with George Zimmerman's killing of Trayvon Martin in 2013. Although the #BlackLivesMatter hashtag was coined during the fallout after Martin's death in 2013, our analysis begins with the fatal shooting of an unarmed Black teenager by a white police officer in the St. Louis suburb of Ferguson on August 9, 2014. This event captured national and international attention in the days, weeks, and months that followed through the images and commentary taking place on social media. As the hashtag #Ferguson trended on Twitter, legacy media outlets followed the social media activity around the protests, the militarized police response, and calls for social justice.

A similar event occurred in Cincinnati's Over-the-Rhine neighborhood in 2001 after a white police officer shot and killed an unarmed

Black teenager. However, this was before mobile telecommunications and social media developed into what it was in the mid-2010s, and the protests taking place in Cincinnati only garnered national attention for a few days.

While some critics praised social media for sustaining interest in the events taking place in #Ferguson, others blamed it for prolonging civil unrest in the area. Nonetheless, everyone seemed to agree that social media made a difference.

For instance, the power of social media to disrupt legacy journalistic routines was described by Alfred Hermida in a number of news stories where activity on Twitter outpaced traditional outlets, including the 2009 Iranian election in which tweets about the disputed elections results peaked at over 221,000 in just one hour.[1] Earlier in 2009, Janis Krums's historic picture taken with his iPhone and posted to Twitter immediately after a US Airways commercial flight that made an emergency landing in the Hudson River of New York literally crashed the TwitPic servers due to the high number of views of the image.[2] While this moment has nothing to do with social justice, it was a watershed moment for the shift away from the traditional gatekeeping function of legacy news media. People without formal media credentials were no longer strictly confined to the role of audience. For good or bad, the power of professional journalists in the public sphere was diminished. While this shift in power was useful to social justice advocates who were previously without such a potent platform for their narratives, it also had negative long-term effects on the credibility of journalists reporting thoughtfully on social justice movements and politics. But more on that later.

The immediate impact of social media on social justice movements was, perhaps, first seen in Guatemala after the 2009 murder of Rodrigo Rosenberg in which the victim appeared in a video recorded before (but released after) his death, which blamed President Alvaro Colom for his killing. The video quickly spread on Facebook and YouTube, sparking groups to mobilize on social media. In a content analysis of some of the related Facebook pages, Summer Harlow found that user "comments were framed to mobilize and advance an online justice movement" that also developed into offline protests and civic action, decrying the violence.[3] Harlow concluded that Facebook offered outraged Guatemalans a forum to express opinions, organize, mobilize, and act as citizen journalists by documenting protests and activities—thus bypassing the traditional gatekeeping function of mainstream news media. While the Guatemalans that Harlow interviewed were mixed in their views about the potential role of social media in social movements, the so-called Arab Spring, which occurred two years later, would further demonstrate its significance.[4]

In a comprehensive study that included a database of social media data from Facebook, Twitter, and YouTube, Philip Howard and colleagues found that social media played an integral role in the Arab Spring of 2011.[5] Conversations about revolutionary actions would take place on social media before those events would occur, and social media helped to spread information about those events across international boundaries. As social media activity and protests against repressive regimes in Tunisia and Egypt rose, those governments fell. The wave of protests and organization on social media then swept across other parts of North Africa and the Middle East as organizers and advocates for greater democracy in those regions used social media to circumvent state-controlled media. Moreover, how the Arab Spring played out on social media fostered "transnational links between individuals and groups" allowing social justice movements to tell "compelling stories . . . in short text messages or long video documentaries."[6] Western journalists then picked up these stories from social media and carried them to audiences on traditional news outlets.

Hermida, Lewis, and Zamith looked at the intersection of journalism and activism on Twitter as a place where activists and journalists make news together. Their case study focused on NPR journalist Andy Carvin's coverage of the Egyptian and Tunisian uprisings on Twitter, and his selection of sources in the coverage. Hermida, Lewis, and Zamith found that Carvin used a significant number of "nonelite" or alternative sources on Twitter, giving credence to the claim that social media broadens the scope of voices in the media in general.[7]

While the Arab Spring successfully demonstrated the role of social media in allowing people to document protests and provided commentary outside of the gatekeeping of traditional news media, the Occupy Wall Street movement that started in September 2011 near New York City's financial district to protest corporate corruption and governmental influence provided further illustration of social media's power to engage individuals not directly (or physically) involved in on-the-ground demonstrations. As Kevin DeLuca, Sean Lawson, and Ye Sun showed, the Occupy Wall Street movement created a context for both collective activism and perceptual participation, both of which occurred outside the mainstream news media.[8] That is, rather that only relying on news reporting about protest activities from a more neutral perspective, activists and outside observers could interact with each other about the meaning and significance of their activities and the movement at large.

Additionally, the Occupy Wall Street movement showed the strategic potential for Twitter to enhance the visibility and symbolic power of social justice efforts. Rong Wang and Winlin Liu examined Twitter data during a two-day period of Occupy Wall Street and found that strategic combinations of viral hashtags by users would mobilize public figures and other influential actors towards the movement.[9] Using Karine Nahon and Jeff Hemsley's "virality" framework that describes the flow of specific social information within one's own social network, as well as "distant networks, resulting in a sharp acceleration in the number of people who are exposed to the message" within a short period of time,[10] Wang, Liu, and Gao found that the tweets with powerful social messages had the ability to "go viral" and were helpful in making a networked social movement more prominent.[11]

More than just going viral, though, social media platforms have become an important venue for self-definition of otherwise marginalized voices. For instance, following a string of murders and suicides of LGBTQ youth in 2012, Janet Mock engaged her "cultural capital" through the use of YouTube videos and supportive hashtags such as #GirlsLikeUs, to advocate for trans women.[12] In China, LGBTQ people used the microblogging social media outlet Weibo to generate alternative discourses about sexual orientation and challenge government censorship under the #IAmGay# tag.[13] In the U.S., feminist social movements have engaged in hashtag activism, such as #MeToo, to give voice to an array of social and political problems.[14]

What connects these disparate social justice movements for the purpose of analysis here is their use of social media platforms to engage with a broader group of like-minded strangers, making a somewhat headless network to address some form of social change. Admittedly, these are massive and quickly changing arenas, which can be analyzed through a number of different frameworks. Clay Shirky provided one of the first more comprehensive examinations of people using social media tools, such as MySpace, Twitter, and Flickr, to do things without traditional organizational structures. Shirky noted that social media platforms broke down traditional barriers of time and cost in communication among a large body of people.[15] Similarly, Lee Rainie and Barry Wellman presented online social networks as liberating and empowering in what they described as "networked individualism" in a "triple revolution" of social networking, internet capacity, and constant connectivity of mobile devices.[16] Rather than relying on tight-knit in-person groups for networking, individuals now had ever-present mobile devices and online sources to connect them professionally, socially, and informationally with a wider array of other individuals and groups.

However, Shirky tempered some of these networked utopian sentiments and observed that the components of interaction among social media networks were complex and did not guarantee the success of a group's objectives. Shirky also warned of the "mass amateurization" of journalism that would change the way news is spread.[17] In a similar vein, Zeynep Tufekci raised concerns about the ultimate fate of networked movements in the face of perplexing contradictions, such as the concurrent rise of empowering social technologies along with authoritarian regimes, as well as the spread of misinformation on social media being more effective than outright censorship at squelching the voices of social justice advocates.[18] For instance, a Twitter account belonging to the white nationalist group Identity Evropa falsely claimed that it represented "antifa" during protests over George Floyd's killing by a police officer in Minneapolis.[19] The account handle, "@ANTIFA_US" attempted to incite violence while unfairly placing the blame on social justice advocates. As this example shows, there is more to the story of how social justice activity on social media plays out. While social media platforms can strengthen otherwise weak interpersonal ties into informal networks of common purpose, understanding how human relationships form on social media around causes of social justice is only part of the dynamic that warrants scholarly investigation, as these networks are also shaped by larger political and economic forces, including misinformation, manipulation, and deception.

Our book enters this body of scholarship to provide a comprehensive examination of how politics and financial organization of social media networks effect the production and distribution of content on these platforms, as well as the relationship between social media (particularly Twitter) in contemporary social justice movements and political engagements. In addition to exploring the intended use of social media by social justice advocates, this work will also look at how commercial interests (through the use of bots and people posting and re-Tweeting items simply to "get clicks") shape discourse about social justice and politics, and will examine efforts to sow disinformation.

Our initial study focused exclusively on the #BlackLivesMatter social justice cases related to #Ferguson.[20] This took an unexpected turn after the U.S. presidential election in 2016, in which Russian-based operations exploited social media platforms with the intention of influencing political sentiments among different groups of Americans. Naturally, we wondered about how troll accounts, bots, and other forms of digital manipulation might have been employed amid some of the social justice events we were studying, and how these fit into election politics and the broader political economy of online social media networks.

Our scope broadened, similarly to what Kate Starbird described about a University of Washington study of the way in which "framing contests" emerged on social media about #BlackLivesMatter.[21] That is, how were different groups of people and political interests trying to describe the meaning of the #BlackLivesMatter social movement (e.g., a broad-based and grassroots efforts to call attention to social injustices in policing; or a singular group of radical Marxists)? After the U.S. House Intelligence Committee in November 2017 released a list of Twitter accounts that were the product of Russia's Internet Research Agency during the 2016 election cycle, Starbird's team realized that several of these accounts were ones that had been active in the #BlackLivesMatter conversations they had been studying. Specifically, tweets that Starbird's team had been analyzing were not created by "real" #BlackLivesMatter activists or #BlueLivesMatter proponents; they were instead products of the Russian-based Internet Research Agency. As Starbird explained, this revelation underscored the power and nuance of manipulative strategies online:

> These IRA agents were enacting caricatures of politically active U.S. citizens. In some cases, these were gross caricatures of the worst kinds of online actors, using the most toxic rhetoric. But, in other cases, these accounts appeared to be everyday people like us, people who care about the things we care about, people who want the things we want, people who share our values and frames. [22]

Moreover, as Starbird's group discovered, Russian-based trolls had been involved in an array of U.S.-based political conversations through social media, including gun rights, immigration, and others. The point being that some of the "frames" created to understand the meaning of #BlackLivesMatter were artificially generated to enhance political divisions or undermine the broader movement by making it appear to be something menacing.

While Starbird's team kept their subsequent research focused on frames and Russian manipulation of frames, our approach has broadened to understand various forms of influence on social media networks, including trolling activity and bullying from a variety of actors, the use of bots, as well as tweet and retweet relationships, to understand how social networks form and may be gamed. Altogether, this intersection of voices (real and fake), technology, economic concerns, and social networks forming online creates an epistemic environment that is fraught with difficulty for advocates of social justice.

The first part of this book is a big-data analysis of social justice movements at the global and local scales on Twitter, and our primary test case is #BlackLivesMatter and related hashtags that were invoked in the aftermath of the Mike Brown shooting in the St. Louis suburb of Ferguson in 2014. The purpose of this initial part of our study is to provide an overview of the semantic discourse—the meaning of the millions of tweets—that defined the social movement globally and to examine the story elements that people tend to focus on through their use of specific hashtags. From this analysis it appears that the conversation on Twitter tended to focus on the personal meaning of story events and framed the shooting as something relatable to the posters' own lives and experiences.

Our analysis continues by applying and comparing the lessons of social media messaging in the Ferguson case to on-the-ground social justice activities in Cincinnati led by @BlackLivesMatterCincy and their efforts surrounding the Sam DuBose shooting. When examining the significance of social media in shaping political discourse about events and activities related to social justice efforts, it becomes apparent that social justice movements would be well served to include media reform strategies into their efforts.

The second part of our book moves to a broader discussion about political discourse on social media, especially in relation to Twitter trolls, cyber-bullying, harassment, misinformation, and other behavior patterns that can undercut social justice groups' efforts to effectively engage in political conversations taking shape online. The section focuses on Twitter activity during the 2016 U.S. presidential election cycle when concerns came to the fore about the impact that fake news, bots, and propaganda campaigns had in shaping political dialogue.

The third and final section of our analysis brings together an examination of social justice activities and varying narratives about these movements. How do cultural politics inform these narratives? How does the organization, structure, and financial interests of social media platforms shape these narratives? We aim to address these questions through a critically informed and morally based philosophic perspective. Our goal is to contribute to an ongoing scholarly discussion about the interplay between online social networks, culture, politics, economics, and social justice. This scholarly discussion includes Christian Fuch's book, *Culture and Economy in the Age of Social Media*,[23] which examined the culturally based meaning that groups of people apply to the use of social media, as well as looking at how social media platforms are organized for financial profit, and the subsequent impact of that imperative on culture and the economy. Another important voice in this conversation is Zizi Papacharissi and her book, *Affective Publics: Sentiment, Technology and Politics*, which provided an insightful analysis of the effect that streams of Twitter conversations can have within larger political debates.[24] From our analysis, the political economic struggle that is taking place throughout online networks can be seen as two opposing forces of social justice efforts from the bottom up, and social propaganda from the top down, as well as other artificially created communities, in which social networks' business models generate links between people. Here we apply Edward Herman and Noam Chomsky's class propaganda model to the digital marketplace of ideas and find that too often grassroots movements can be manufactured from the top down via social media networks, confounding social justice movements and confusing epistemic validity within political discourse.[25]

chapter 3

social media power
in #ferguson

Our first case explores the relationship between social media and social justice movements, as social media and mobile streaming applications provide a potent form of storytelling power to users across the communicative landscape. How do social media platforms, such as Twitter, affect public discourse about social justice? Notably, perhaps, social media platforms have the potential to change the relationship between news media and the public in significant ways, as virtually everyone now has the ability to document and livestream events to a global audience. As noted earlier, social media has become a primary venue for public commentary about current events and has disrupted some of the gatekeeping power once held by national news outlets and talk radio in the discussion of public affairs.

Some of the most poignant examples of this restructuring of communicative power can be seen in social justice movements and the instant release of imagery and commentary in the wake of multiple shootings of Black men by police officers across the U.S. in recent years. For instance, Diamond Reynolds livestreamed the moments after the shooting of her fiancé, Philando Castile, when they were pulled over by police for a broken taillight in Falcon Heights, Minnesota.[1] Videos were posted online when police in Baton Rouge shot Alton Sterling, prompting an investigation from the U.S. Justice Department. As mentioned earlier, civil unrest followed the shooting of Michael Brown, an unarmed Black teenager in the St. Louis suburb of Ferguson in the summer of 2014. As the hashtag #Ferguson trended on Twitter, national and international news outlets followed social media activity in covering the protests, looting, and militarized police response. And in Cincinnati during the summer of 2015, Sam DuBose, an unarmed Black motorist, was shot and killed during a traffic stop by a University of Cincinnati police officer. Afterwards, local community groups led by @BlackLivesCincy and @theIRATE8 quickly mobilized on social media to decry the incident and confront competing narratives that it was justified.

In this chapter we engage in a big-data analysis of #BlackLivesMatter and related hashtags that were invoked on Twitter in the aftermath of the Mike Brown shooting in the St. Louis suburb of Ferguson in 2014. The purpose of this chapter is to present not only a broad overview of Twitter activity and viral hashtags after the event, but moreover, to build off our previous examination of affective discourse within the millions of tweets that defined the social movement related to the killing of unarmed Black men at the hands of police officers.[2] In that study, we focused more closely on how social media platforms, such as Twitter, can elevate the voices of communities who are affected by an event but who would otherwise be without communicative power. However, the findings presented here show how social justice groups in general, and the public in particular, use social media to provide a more diverse array of commentary about the meaning and implications of civic activity; they also indicate how historically marginalized groups and the broader public have exercised their First Amendment rights in ways that have redefined the relationship between public communication, national news outlets, and international networks. Furthermore, our analysis of tweets in the aftermath of the Mike Brown shooting and the non-indictment of Darren Wilson show that individual posters tended to relate the meaning of these events to their own lives and framed these events as relatable to a broader array of personal experiences and events.

Deen Freelon, Charlton McIlwain, and Meredith Clark suggested that the internet in general, especially Twitter, were instrumental in developing the Black Lives Matter movement. Although the #BlackLivesMatter hashtag was generated in the summer of 2013 after George Zimmerman was acquitted for the murder of Trayvon Martin, according to Freelon, McIlwain, and Clark it was not a popular one until August 2014, when it was frequently invoked during the Ferguson protests.[3] Other studies have further detailed how social justice movements have effectively engaged social media in general, and Twitter in particular, to provide counter-narratives to legacy news media, to intensify public debate and criticism about law enforcement, as well as to yield more in-depth dialogue on and personalization of the issues.

Although their study was not specifically related to the Black Lives Matter movement, Sarah Jackson and Brooke Welles showed that minority voices have used Twitter to establish effective counter-narratives challenging police activity that extend into mainstream media.[4] Ryan Gallagher, Andrew Reagan, Christopher Danforth, and Peter Dodds found in their analysis of 800,000 tweets the #BlackLivesMatter hashtag amplified public criticism of police killings of unarmed Black men.[5] Moreover, users invoking the #BlackLivesMatter hashtag tended to have more "informationally rich conversations" than their counter-parts who used the #AllLivesMatter hashtag.[6] Those posters using the #BlackLivesMatter hashtag demonstrated more diversity in word usage, and cut across topic networks more frequently, comparison to tweets featuring the #AllLivesMatter hashtag. Alexandra Olteanu, Ingmar Weber, and Daniel Gatica-Perez reached a similar conclusion, showing that Black people who use the #BlackLivesMatter hashtag are more likely to engage the ethical dimensions and personal implications of sensitive topics.[7]

Freelon, McIlwain, and Clark analyzed tweets from a year-long time period (June 1, 2014 to May 31, 2015), which included events over two months before the Michael Brown shooting, and nearly a year after, and other studies have explored the #BlackLivesMatter phenomenon on social media more broadly.[8] However, the examination presented here focused on tweets from specific time periods related to the Mike Brown shooting (the immediate aftermath of the shooting itself, and the non-indictment of Officer Wilson) when interest and emotions were arguably highest, to better understand the story elements that individuals tend to tweet about for a defined event. The purpose of Freelon, McIlwain, and Clark's research was to study the Black Lives Matter organization, which used the #BlackLivesMatter hashtag, but the hashtag itself was not the focus of the study. Additionally, their report covered Black Lives Matter's involvement in an array of cases, including ones involving Eric Garner, Mike Brown, Walter Scott, and Freddie Gray.[9] However, our data presented in this chapter focus on an array of hashtags for just two distinct time periods related to a single event (the immediate aftermath of the Mike Brown shooting, and after the non-indictment of Darren Wilson three months later).

The time periods noted here are ripe for analysis of the role of social media in social justice movements. Social media provided instantaneous imagery and commentary in the civil unrest that followed the shooting, and moreover, as the hashtag #Ferguson trended on Twitter, national news outlets seemed to be following social media activity in covering the protests, looting, and militarized police response. It is clear based on the cases presented in Guatemala, the Arab Spring, Occupy Wall Street, Black Lives Matter, and Ferguson, as well as feminist, trans, and more recent LGBTQ movements in China that social media provided a powerful platform for previously unheard voices. Papacharissi explained this kind of phenomenon as "affective expression" in the form of networked publics who "want to tell their story collaboratively and on their own terms."[10] That is, social media is a venue for people to demonstrate their proximity (e.g., closeness to, or distance from) to events, political movements, and other social experiences. Groups of people more closely affected by certain experiences now have communicative power that is at least equal to others who are less personally involved. Moreover, these "affective publics" tend to "produce disruptions . . . of dominant political narratives by presencing [sic] underrepresented viewpoints."[11] From this review of literature on social justice movements, social media have presented significant opportunities for the disturbance and redirection of dominant and oppressive narratives.

To better understand the "affective publics" described by Papacharissi for the social network analysis in this study, we adapted Robert Entman's approach to studying media frames, or how the selection and editing of particular story elements tend to focus audience attention. This approach understands that media-based narratives of an event or issue convey meaning through their creation, specifically the selection of and emphasis on certain story elements.[12] Based on the national and international attention about the role social media (especially Twitter) played in the aftereffects of the events of Ferguson, the overarching goal of our research project was to understand which story elements people were focusing on in their tweets and hashtags, as well as how these platforms gave voice to underrepresented publics.

While previous research has broadly explained how social justice movements have effectively engaged social media in general and Twitter in particular to provide counternarratives to legacy news media and to intensify public debate and criticism of law enforcement apparatuses, our examination evaluates the most used and impactful hashtags in the immediate aftermath of a specific event (the Michael Brown shooting in Ferguson). We also examine changes over time, including triggering events where the hashtags originally invoked during the immediate aftermath of the shooting might spike again, such as the legal decision to not indict police officer Darren Wilson for the killing. Specifically, we asked the following sets of research questions:

What were the most used and impactful hashtags in the immediate aftermath of the Mike Brown shooting in Ferguson? Moreover, what were the broader social and political takeaways from this event and subsequent social media activity? What was the broader impact on the public sphere and social discourse around Black rights and the racial issues with law enforcement? This set of questions entails both data analytics and a qualitative component. First, we wanted to know which hashtags went viral and were used most frequently in tweets. Second, we wanted a qualitative assessment of the meaning and implications of those most popular hashtags. What kinds of messages (or frames) did they convey?

Did they focus on places and names in the story (as an event), or did they provide commentary, a call for action, or something else?

We also wanted to examine change over time by analyzing what we imagined would be triggering events where the hashtags (invoked during the immediate aftermath of the shooting) might spike again, including legal decisions such as Darren Wilson's non-indictment. We wanted to know which were the most used and resonant hashtags after the non-indictment, which again requires both data analytics and qualitative analysis: which hashtags were used most frequently after Darren Wilson was not indicted, and what were the meaning and implications of those hashtags? Rather than understanding social media activity as being limited just to the events of Ferguson, our analysis showed that posters were relating what happened in Ferguson to other racial issues involving unarmed Black people and police.

As described in Blevins, Lee, McCabe, and Edgerton, we took every tweet from across the globe posted in the four months after the Michael Brown shooting from the open-source Twitter historical archive related to #BLM, and created a network showing which users and regions responded to one another during that intense period from August 2014 (the month of the Michael Brown police shooting) to December 2014 (the aftermath of the Darren Wilson non-indictment).[13]

From this time period, we extracted hashtags, tweets, and retweets from the Twitter archive in order to explore tweet-retweet relationships, and generate basic descriptive statistics about tweets and hashtags. The nodes in the data sets represent individual Twitter users and the links you see are built between those users and others who retweeted them. In this process, we preserve important data, such as tweet text and time of tweet, for more detailed exploration. These nodes and links can also be filtered by time.

Data set # 1: Hashtag frequency/time chart (August 2014)
https://themlmom.com/projects/blm?type=basic-aug
Data set # 2: Tweets by hour (August 2014)
https://themlmom.com/projects/blm?type=networks-aug
Data set # 3: Hashtag frequency/time chart (November–December 2014)
https://themlmom.com/projects/blm?type=basic-novdec
Data set # 4: Tweets by hour (November–December 2014)
https://themlmom.com/projects/blm?type=networks-novdec

Scan this QR code for the online version of Chapter 3, where you can view the live links for these datasets

Note that in Data set # 1 the most popular hashtags are proper names of the victim (e.g., #MikeBrown and #MichaelBrown). Other place and proper names used in hashtags (e.g., #FergusonPolice, #DarrenWilson, and #EricGarner) were less interesting in our view, as they merely referenced a basic element of the story (a person or a place). Hashtags such as #AllLivesMatter, #BlackLivesMatter, and #JusticeforMikeBrown can be considered as ideological markers because they indicated a particular position (or belief) about the event. #JusticeforMikeBrown is the most popular of these, and it also includes the proper name of the victim in the hashtag. We considered hashtags, such as #IfTheyGunnedMeDown and #ICantBreathe as conceptual markers because they make personal conceptualizations of (or references to) the story. Interestingly, #IfTheyGunnedMeDown was the most popular of these in the early weeks after the shooting. In a short amount of time, people were making the shooting a more personalized issue, rather than referencing it as a separate, single event.

In Data set # 2 we found that hashtags with proper names (e.g., #MikeBrown) were most prominent in the first wave of Twitter activity and are the first hashtags that go viral. However, more conceptual markers, such as #IfTheyGunnedMeDown, and ideological tags, like #BlackLivesMatter, register only faint activity in the immediate aftermath of the Michael Brown shooting.

By November of 2014 (a few months after the shooting), in Data set # 3 and near the announcement of Darren Wilson's non-indictment in the shooting, more conceptual markers, such as #IfTheyGunnedMeDown and #ICantBreathe, which include personalization of the issues, dominate the Twitter network along with #MikeBrown. We examined change over time by analyzing triggering events where the hashtags spike again (e.g., Darren Wilson's non-indictment) and the Eric Garner death. By this point, conceptual hashtags like #BlackLivesMatter and #ICantBreathe have eclipsed #MikeBrown.

Furthermore, in Data set # 4 #IfTheyGunnedMeDown is a far more popular hashtag at times and does not always share links to #MikeBrown. Here the two markers appear to be independent, with little to no correlation in their activity. As ideological hashtags such as #BlackLivesMatter and #ICantBreathe eclipsed #MikeBrown, the #EricGarner marker appeared to have a multiplier effect—amplifying activity on the Ferguson-related hashtags. Several months after the Michael Brown shooting, and in the wake of the legal decision to not indict Darren Wilson, the hashtags are much more interconnected and correlate to one another.

Textual Analysis of Hashtags

Based on the unexpected dominance of conceptual tags such as #IfTheyGunnedMeDown, we did a qualitative textual analysis of the use and significance of some of these hashtags. One of the more notable elements of these hashtags is that they included first-person personalization of the issue. Using the hashtag #IfTheyGunnedMeDown, individuals juxtaposed two dissimilar images of themselves: one, a wholesome picture of the individual, perhaps attired in cap and gown at a high school graduation; the other, the same person in street attire, maybe holding an alcoholic beverage or cigarette. The question being: if the police killed me, which picture would be in the news—the wholesome high school graduate, or the menace to society? By featuring two contrasting images of the same person, these posts demonstrated that one picture alone does not tell the whole story of a person; and questioned the tendency of news media to focus on the one image that contributes to the "menace to society" narrative.

In reaction to eyewitness accounts that Brown was surrendering with his hands up before being shot, several posts on Twitter using the hashtag #HandsUpDontShoot featured images of people holding their hands up. One of the most potent was a video of kids on a school bus chanting: "Hands up, don't shoot." The message suggested that Michael Brown "could have been me," and engages concern about police officers overestimating the threat posed by Black suspects, and too quickly responding with deadly force.

Social media appeared to change the relationship between news media and the public, as tweets and posts went beyond reiterating the images and messages from traditional news outlets about the events in Ferguson. Rather, social media was the platform for people in Ferguson to document what was happening to a global audience, and the primary venue for public commentary. For instance, the conversation from (and about) Ferguson reached as far as the Middle East, where Palestinians tweeted in solidarity about racial injustice.[14] Several players for the then-St. Louis Rams attracted international attention when they came onto the field before a National Football League game imitating the #HandsUpDontShoot thread on Twitter.[15] Social justice advocates were able to help drive the local, national, and international conversation through social media.

From this broader qualitative examination, it appears that social media provided a forum for both a community in Ferguson and the public at large to tell its own stories in the aftermath of the shooting and challenge the images that tend to pervade national news. In a mediated world dominated by national outlets, social media allowed the public to exercise its First Amendment rights in a way that changed the balance of communicative power and enhanced everyone's ability to relate the meaning of the events in Ferguson to their own personal lives.

The data visualizations presented here bring shape to our understanding of social movements and political action as it plays out on social media. For instance, our network visualizations provide a more visceral form of what a "social movement" may look like as it develops on social media, compared to more conventional appearances in terms of strikes, protest marches, and sit-ins.

Moreover, the visualization of movements taking place on Twitter can reshape our understanding of how political action takes place in the digital era. We have used network analysis techniques to track how social justice hashtags attain a "viral" status, and have found that factual and descriptive hashtags, including proper names such as #MikeBrown and place names such as #Ferguson, are the first wave of hashtags that become viral. More conceptual and ideological markers, like #BLM, registered only faint activity in the immediate aftermath of the Michael Brown shooting. But after one to two weeks, they dominated the discourse and captured more media attention. In examining change in the hashtag behavior over time by analyzing triggering events where the hashtags register large increases in activity, legal decisions such as Darren Wilson's non-indictment, and the death of Eric Garner, appeared to have contributed to greater personalization of the events.

The results of this study support Papacharissi's explanation of social media activity as an affective form of expression for groups and individuals about social justice issues.[16] By telling their own stories, on their own terms (as indicated by the conceptual hashtags) these "affective publics" disrupted the power typically held by mainstream news outlets, and in the process, changed the conversation from one that focuses on basic story elements (people, places, and events) to one in which the meaning of the event is more internalized (e.g., #IfTheyGunnedMeDown and #ICantBreathe). What is unique in the aftermath of the Mike Brown shooting is that the most meaningful hashtags were the ones that helped to frame the shooting as something relatable to the posters' own lives and experiences. These conceptual hashtags framed the event as something

personal—if "I" were gunned down, "I" can't breathe, and so on. Twitter
users did more than use the platform to simply comment on an event
(#MikeBrownShooting) that occurred at a particular place (#Ferguson);
and even more than reinforcing popular ideological frames (e.g.,
#BlackLivesMatter v. #BlueLivesMatter). Rather, the conceptual frame
presented in the #IfIWereGunnedDown hashtag was more dynamic—it
personalized the issue for both Black and white individuals. In the jux-
taposition of images of single persons, Black people showed that police
and legacy media tend to unfairly characterize them based on appearance, whereas white people demonstrated an awareness of their own
privilege—that in similar situations, police and media do not make the
same assumptions. The employment of personal conceptual frames in
hashtags is ripe for further qualitative analysis in other cases.

For advocates of social justice, we would also caution that social
media, as a platform, is not just about liberating the voices of the
marginalized. Papacharissi's explanation of affective expression of networked publics can also be applied to hate groups.[17] While social media
has helped social justice advocates to be more effective storytellers, it
also empowers hate groups and others who use these digital tools as
forms of intimidation through trolling, cyberbullying, and social media
mobbing, in which targets are relentlessly barraged with insults, threats,
and vulgar memes intending to drown out more respectful voices in the
process.[18] How social media can be used to disrupt social justice efforts,
empower hateful expression, or practice intimidation is also deserving
of further scholarly attention from communication researchers.

Furthermore, the set of visualization and text-mining tools on social
media data employed in this study can transcend social justice applications, and we envision that our social network analysis method can
have broad applications across disciplines. In developing the project
presented here and its results, we make the machine learning algorithms
that we have applied to the Twitter archive, as well as the visualizations
we developed from the data, accessible on a cloud platform as online
research tools for scholars and students to analyze social justice hashtags
and the social media discourse at a big-data scale.

While the data presented in this chapter shed light on how discourse about social justice takes shape on Twitter, it does not address the context of the on-the-ground efforts of social justice advocates and how social media is but one part of their media strategy. Our next chapter explores some of the historical background of social justice movements in their struggle and relationship with legacy news outlets to deepen our understanding of social media's significance in the present landscape.

chapter 4

Affected and Effective @BlackLivesMatterCincy

We now take a deeper look at how social media platforms affect public discourse about social justice by looking at what happened with another locally based BLM movement, @BlackLivesMatterCincy. Almost a year after the Mike Brown shooting in Ferguson, another shooting of an unarmed Black man at the hands of a white police officer engaged a local community on social media platforms. A similar motif seemed to play out in local news coverage in Cincinnati following the 2015 shooting of Sam DuBose, an unarmed black motorist, who was killed during a traffic stop by Ray Tensing, a white University of Cincinnati police officer. Shortly afterwards, local community groups led by @BlackLivesCincy and @theIRATE8 quickly mobilized on social media to decry the incident and confront competing narratives that it was justified. They continued to utilize multiple social media platforms in a sustained effort that involved a broader array of social justice issues beyond the DuBose shooting. Again, social media had emerged as a critical venue for social justice discourse and activity, especially for Black people in the U.S. as control over legacy media outlets have become increasingly concentrated, with few minority owners.[1]

This chapter provides an in-depth interview with two social justice leaders in Cincinnati about their social media strategies following the shooting of a Black motorist by a University of Cincinnati police officer. Additionally, we explore how legacy news outlets in Cincinnati covered the @BlackLivesMatterCincy group that mobilized after the shooting, and provide a critical examination of access to Internet, mobile media, and legacy news among low-income groups that shapes social justice efforts in significant ways. Accordingly, we examine the need for social justice activists to adopt media reform strategies.

As Rachel Mourao and colleagues showed in their content analysis of five newspapers during the first wave of protests in Ferguson after the Mike Brown shooting, "initial stories were predominantly episodic and focused on violence to the detriment of demands and grievances" expressed by social justice advocates.[2] While the newspaper coverage was also critical of the militaristic police response, and eventually addressed issues related to race and police brutality, Mourao and colleagues concluded that newspapers should provide more "contextual narratives behind social movements' actions," rather than focusing on protester activities and police response.[3]

Similarly, Daniele Kilgo and colleagues argued that "mainstream media's narrative choices marginalize and delegitimize protesters and their causes," and their longitudinal content analysis of national newspaper reporting showed that coverage before the judicial rulings in the Trayvon Martin and Michael Brown cases "focused on protesters' tactics (violence versus peaceful)" and only moved to the realm of understanding ideas about grievances after the assailants were cleared of legal wrongdoing.[4]

To explore local news coverage of the Sam Dubose shooting in Cincinnati we conducted a Boolean search of keywords on the websites for legacy outlets from the period of July 2015 (when the shooting occurred) through November 2016 (when Tensing was acquitted of charges of murder). Our search terms were "Sam Dubose," "Black Lives Matter," "Black Lives Matter Cincinnati" and "Irate8." The news organizations covered were *The Cincinnati Enquirer* (the city's daily newspaper), *CityBeat* (the alt-weekly paper), as well as television stations WXIX-TV (the city's FOX affiliate) and WCPO-TV (the city's ABC affiliate). We excluded from analysis the city's African-American newspaper, *The Cincinnati Herald*, as well as the city's other network-affiliated television stations (WKRC-TV, CBS, and WLWT-TV, NBC) due to the limited functionality of conducting keyword searches on their websites. Our content analysis showed the following mentions in each outlet:

News media	Sam Dubose	Black Lives Matter	Black Lives Matter Cincinnati	Irate8
The Enquirer	90	18	13	1
CityBeat	37	9	7	3
WXIX-TV	43	10	2	0
WCPO-TV	99	22	11	1

Figure 4.1
Keyword mentions in Cincinnati legacy news: July 2016–November 2016

A couple of interesting points may be noted here: First, newspapers were more likely to distinguish "Black Lives Matter Cincinnati" (the local group in their reporting) from the more general reference "Black Lives Matter." *The Enquirer* and *CityBeat* mentioned the local organization in 15.7 percent of their stories, compared to 9 percent for WXIX and WCPO combined. Furthermore, *The Enquirer* and *CityBeat* mentioned Black Lives Matter Cincinnati (20 references) almost as often as Black Lives Matter (27 references), while WXIX and WCPO more often referred to Black Lives Matter (32 references) than Black Lives Matter Cincinnati (13 references). Meanwhile, the Irate 8 student group was only mentioned a total of five times across all four outlets, three of which were in *CityBeat*.

However, in reading through each of the 269 stories across the 4 media outlets, *CityBeat* tended to use "Black Lives Matter Cincinnati" and "Black Lives Matter" interchangeably, or simply used the term "activists" to umbrella the organizations under one entity. *CityBeat* did mention past cases of police brutality in Cincinnati and other U.S. cities such as Ferguson and Baltimore, thereby providing some national context, similar to the tweets in the Ferguson case (as described in Chapter 2). In 12 of *CityBeat*'s 37 articles about the Sam DuBose shooting, there was at least some reference to a history of police brutality in Cincinnati, or other U.S. cities.

Only 4 of WXIX's 43 media stories about the Dubose shooting contain some mention of past police brutality in Cincinnati or the U.S. Furthermore, WXIX rarely mentioned "Black Lives Matter Cincinnati" (two mentions), and never mentioned the Irate 8 in its coverage. Rather, the station tended to use blanket terms, such as "protestors" and "demonstrators." The effect of these kinds of generic expressions is that they tend to (even unintentionally) minimize the significance of a specific movement taking shape. The lack of recognition for newly (or less) established groups promoting nascent causes is also an impediment for group identity and messaging in legacy news outlets.

A noted feature in WCPO and *The Enquirer*'s coverage was that both outlets often noted that "Black Lives Matter" or "Black Lives Matter Cincinnati" organized a rally (or march) in an article's headline or photo cutlines, but would not specifically call the activity an event organized by Black Lives Matter or Black Lives Matter Cincinnati in the actual article. In one case, an article included a tweet that depicted a poster for an event honoring Sam DuBose, which read "Organized by the family of Sam DuBose, Black Lives Matter Cincinnati, and the Irate 8." However, the article only stated that the DuBose family would hold the event. Other articles would mention that Black Lives Matter Cincinnati scheduled a rally, but the follow-up article would not mention who organized the event.

Both WCPO and *The Enquirer* often referred to Black Lives Matter supporters as "protestors," and photos showing Black Lives Matter Cincinnati members did not mention the group in the cutlines. Similar to *CityBeat* and FOX19, WCPO and *The Enquirer* used "Black Lives Matter" and "Black Lives Matter Cincinnati" interchangeably. For example, WCPO referred to Brian Taylor as a "Black Lives Matter" organizer instead of a "Black Lives Matter Cincinnati" organizer. *The Enquirer* referred to Ashley Harrington and Brian Taylor as "Black Lives Matter" steering committee co-chairs in some articles and "Black Lives Matter Cincinnati" steering committee co-chairs in others. However, similar to *CityBeat* and FOX19, WCPO and *The Enquirer* often mentioned past cases of police brutality in Cincinnati and other U.S. cities in their coverage of Sam DuBose. Overall, the legacy news media in Cincinnati did not provide the kind of dynamic expression found in social media in the Ferguson case discussed earlier in this book.

Of course, this is not to say that media in Cincinnati intentionally sought to delegitimize or undercut locally based social justice efforts. Rather, the omissions are more likely due to the news routines of legacy media, especially local television; breaking news evolves into more complexity than can often be managed in short packages and sound bites. It is also faster and easier to get a broad overview of events as they are happening on the ground from official government sources rather than the individual narratives of those involved. However, the varying perspectives between official sources and the individual involved in breaking news are significant, to say the least, as Andy Carvin demonstrated in his recounting of the media coverage of the Arab Spring.[5] Breaking news coverage on television tends to focus on events as they happen, and being a visual medium, tends to focus on elements of the story that are the most visually stimulating (e.g., groups of people, police lights, etc.). However, this kind of coverage situated within the immediacy of a moment lacks a more in-depth exploration of meaning.

A notable exception to the breaking news–style coverage of protests in Cincinnati was the FOX19 documentary, "Bigger than a moment: Documenting the outcry of our city" that aired in the aftermath of summer protests over the deaths of Breonna Taylor and George Floyd that shook cities across the U.S.[6] The FOX19 documentary originally aired in two parts one evening and is available on the station's website. What is perhaps most noteworthy in FOX19's effort, besides its running time of over 39 minutes (an eternity in television news) is the range and depth of interviews with people across the community, including those on the front lines of social justice activity. While this was an exceptional effort from a legacy news outlet, it came well after the "moment" it examines and is naturally produced from a more traditional sense of news reporting and storytelling. To be clear, this is not an example of bias in any form, but rather, the technical realities of meaningfully creating a substantive documentary. Television news routines are a natural impediment to the production of this kind of reflective and deep coverage because of their otherwise constant emphasis on immediacy in reporting.

The social media activities utilized by @BlackLivesMatterCincy and @theIRATE8 represented the kind of affective expression from people using mobile and Internet-base telecommunications described by Papacharissi, which "want to tell their story collaboratively and on their own terms."[7] Moreover, these "affective publics" tend to "produce disruptions . . . of dominant political narratives by presencing [sic] underrepresented viewpoints." [8] Based on an interview with two social justice organizers in Cincinnati, we explored how social media presented significant opportunities (and some challenges) for people more personally affected by these events to engage in effective social justice efforts.

"The Irate 8" group name refers to the percentage at the time of University of Cincinnati's student body who are Black. The organization launched a website and social media accounts on Twitter (@theIRATE8) and Facebook. Although the shooting death of an unarmed Black motorist during a traffic stop by a white university police officer was the initial focusing event for the group, their scope of concern quickly broadened to include reforming policies on University of Cincinnati's campus, including retention of Black students and increasing faculty diversity. The Irate 8 keeps a log of media coverage of the organization by legacy news outlets, which also provides a record of their impact on civic discourse about social justice issues.

The DuBose shooting was also a focusing event for @BlackLivesCincy, but the group has also addressed a much broader range of social justice issues on its Twitter account and Facebook page, including transgender rights, support for rape survivors, refugee and immigration policy, poverty, healthcare, environmental justice, and many others. Certainly, the organizational acumen of these groups was a primary reason for their successes, but their engagement with social media and utilization of digital media resources to tell their own stories was also an instrumental factor.

A primary concern expressed by two of the leaders of Black Lives Matter Cincinnati (BLMC), Mona Jenkins and Christina Brown (who was also a member of The Irate 8) was the tendency of legacy news media to inaccurately associate people, activities, and statements to their group. In following local news coverage, Brown said that it seemed like "anybody Black and not happy" was associated as "a member of our organization, particularly if they're behaving in a way that's perceived as unlawful."[9] Jenkins added: "Semantically, they're members of Black Lives Matter, when we don't even know who they are."[10] Both Jenkins and Brown expressed frustration over news media coverage that misrepresented BLMC despite the group's efforts to be a disciplined entity of organizers. However, social media played an important role in allowing BLMC to exercise greater control over its own message. Brown said, "when there is something to be said in our name we will say it in our name," and explained that social media allowed the group an immediate form of communication to make its statements more clearly.[11] Rather than getting caught off guard by interview requests from news media, group members can now direct reporters to statements posted on BLMC's social media accounts.

In addition to better message control, social media provided another "avenue of connection" for BLMC, as part of the group's comprehensive approach, which included email, public posters and door-to-door canvasing. However, Jenkins expressed concern about the "digital divide" and noted that many people in the communities they are trying to reach do not have internet access in their homes, and in some cases do not have television.[12] Brown added,

> we have at least a few folks who are like, "how can I find out about what is happening because I don't have a phone, and I don't have a computer." It's sobering to me as a Black person, who still has more access than the majority of Black folks who have lived in the city for generations. Even if we are able to create access to the media that exists, what is it telling us about ourselves? . . . All we see are mug shots and gunshot victims.[13]

Although Brown sees social media as an important part of BLMC's community-building strategy, she said that it is important to "learn more and more about the limitations of digital access of any kind, whether it's the TV or the Internet."[14] One of the drawbacks for social justice groups using social media as an organizing tool is that it affords an easy and often anonymous way for detractors to post threats and hateful messages.

> This is definitely an issue of Facebook, the level of harassment that we receive and the threats of violence. And they're not always direct, but when people post pictures of dead Black folks and say this is what you all deserve . . . I've seen some very vitriolic stuff posted on our accounts . . . it's worth noting that white supremacists from all over the world attack things on our pages, send us messages. We get a lot of hate commentary.[15]

Jenkins added, "We also get a lot of love too."[16] While Brown acknowledged the affirmation BLMC receives from supporters, she stated:

> I think there's an assumption that we do things without putting ourselves at risk and we put ourselves at risk for something greater than ourselves. It's important to note that this not all reward. The reward is in what will come and building people in the process. We are people and threats to harm us are very real.[17]

While there are serious concerns about threats and harassment for social justice group members who are active on social media, and despite the lack of mobile and internet access for low-income community members—social media is a promising venue to advance social justice efforts. The greatest asset that social media provides is a platform for social justice movements to tell their own stories and circumvent some of the framing and filtering functions of traditional news outlets.

However, it is not always possible for local activists to avoid the broader framing from news media and other groups. In 2018 BLMC distanced itself from the wider BLM movement by changing its name to Mass Action for Black Liberation (MABL) and declaring its own agenda.[18] Besides local news media often conflating BLMC with BLM more generally, MABL wanted to distinguish itself from some of BLM's political program.

Nonetheless, social justice groups and the public use social media to provide a more diverse array of commentary about the meaning and implications of civic activity, allowing historically marginalized groups to exercise their First Amendment rights in ways that have disrupted the gatekeeping power once held by national news outlets and international networks. Social media channels have also boosted the livelihood of social justice movements.

The use of mobile streaming video technology (MSVT), such as Facebook Live and Periscope, which can be used with Twitter, has also emerged as important in broadcasting and documenting events of interest to social justice movements.

> MSVTs are best understood as something akin to live broadcast television with two major differences. First, their use of mobile phones to capture and stream good, quality video means that anyone, anywhere, has the ability to become a live video broadcaster so long as they have a capable smartphone, and this represents a significant change in the barriers for entry to live streaming. Second, dissemination of this video is highly decentralized along social network lines, meaning the power to capture audience attention for events such as news has shifted away from the singular format of the television channel such that it now includes distribution along social networks.[19]

While social media have proven to be valuable platforms for social justice movements, it is important to keep in mind that these outlets and MSVTs depend upon broadband telecommunication networks that are subject to the same forces of neoliberal economic philosophy and cultural politics that affected legacy media outlets. Economic and generational disparities may limit access.

The growth and popularity of social media raises an important question about the usefulness of these platforms, and access to broadband technologies that deliver them, to help advance the cause of recent social justice movements. For instance, the Broadband Technology

Opportunities Program (BTOP) was part of the American Recovery and Reinvestment Act of 2009 (ARRA) and provided over $4 billion in federal grants to be administered by the U.S. Department of Commerce and National Telecommunications and Information Administration to help facilitate broadband internet access and adoption in unserved and underserved areas of the U.S., including rural and urban regions. The BTOP grants also presented an opportunity for media reformers to connect their digital justice efforts to the broader social justice movement. For instance, the Detroit-based Allied Media Projects and Philadelphia's Media Mobilizing Project used the occasion to build coalitions among media reformers and social justice groups focused on an array of concerns, including urban housing, worker's rights, and environmental issues, among other causes.[20] However, long-term efforts to sustain broadband access and media diversity in the FCC was cut short by Republicans in the U.S. House of Representatives in 2011 when they passed an amendment to their spending bill defunding Chief Diversity Officer Lloyd's salary at a time when he was working to spread broadband internet access to low-income people.[21] The BTOP funding was a one-time occasion, but as Joshua Breitbart observed:

> it provided an opportunity for an enduring impact on broadband in the United States. In Philadelphia and Detroit, we were able to use the grant-seeking process as a vehicle for visioning and organizing, and for bringing new voices and audiences into the conversation about our shared digital future.[22]

Long-term social justice movements playing out on social media should take note that their efforts should not be divorced from the media reform movement. As Des Freedman and Jonathan Obar recognized:

> We cannot rely on mainstream media to adequately represent our lives as they are lived, to hold power to account and to reflect honestly on the media's own interconnections with established power; we are forced to make our own media.[23]

In today's media-saturated world, social justice endeavors would benefit from communication platforms that allow for access by all, and to all.

However, those committed to media reform for social justice will also need to bear in mind that they will face "formidable challenges," including the following:

> Entrenched commercial interests and media conglomerates; . . . neoliberal governments; a general public often disenfranchised, digitally illiterate and not focused on issues of media reform; and always, the uphill battle of organization, mobilization, and influence.[24]

Furthermore, because Black people and other racial minorities are more likely than whites to rely on mobile broadband services for access to social media applications, they are also more prone to discriminatory marketing practices based upon predictive analytics of their personal data through pay-for-privacy plans, or service tiers required by their broadband providers.[25] Consequently, social justice efforts toward media reform must encompass the principle of network neutrality to provide better access to information and call for greater privacy protection online to help ensure that social justice advocates are not sanctioned for their choice of online activities based on the economic incentives of telecommunication providers.

Still, the "struggles for communication rights are part of a wider challenge to social and economic inequalities and an essential component of a vision for a just and democratic society."[26] Free expression, and the means of free expression, are worth struggling for and they are an essential component of social justice in the digital age. As Bill Moyers said in his keynote address to the 2007 Media Reform Conference in Memphis: "freedom begins the moment you realize someone else has been writing your story, and it's time you took the pen from his hand and started writing it yourself." Furthermore, the principle of free expression is dynamic and includes not only the individual liberty of self-expression, but also the freedom to receive a diverse array of expression from a variety of sources to better inform ourselves about social, economic, political, and cultural matters. When everyone speaks, they do more than just empower themselves—they empower everyone else by making the informational and expressive climate richer, more meaningful, and better informed.

political discourse
on social media, twitter trolls,
and Hashtag Hijacking

While our previous chapters examined the ways in which social media can empower historically disenfranchised groups, racial minorities, and affective networked publics, we now look at the ways in which social media conversations about race turn politically charged and, in many cases, ugly; we will review as well how social justice groups can counteract some of these narratives. A Pew Research Center study by Monica Anderson showed that social media is an important venue for news and political information, while focusing national attention on racially involved issues.

> In fact, two of the most used hashtags around social causes in Twitter history focus on race and criminal justice: #Ferguson and #BlackLivesMatter . . . and key news events . . . often serve as a catalyst for social media conversations about race.[1]

Perhaps less understood, though, is the effective quality of this discourse, and its connection to popular politics, especially when Twitter trolls and social media mobs go on the attack.

Social media mobbing occurs when groups of people converge on Facebook, Twitter, and other social media platforms around an issue that they are angry about, or a person that offends them. The mob relentlessly trolls that person or dominates discussion of the issue with a barrage of insults, arguments, and memes. Some of the more notable targets of social media mobbing have been Black women, including Saturday Night Live comedian Leslie Jones, Olympian Gabby Douglas, and the mother of a young boy who fell into a gorilla exhibit at the Cincinnati Zoo.[2]

This calls into question the quality of public discourse taking place in certain venues on social media. Since there are no universally accepted community standards online, conversations taking place via social media can occasionally escalate into a mob-like atmosphere in which the more even-tempered speakers are heckled off the platform in a rabble of highly offensive posts, including some that are explicitly racist. For instance, Leslie Jones, who used Twitter to speak out against sexism and racism, eventually deleted her account under the crushing emotional strain of the social media mob that was trolling her with crude attacks about her appearance.[3]

In another case, the Cincinnati Zoo asked social media users to stop posting memes about Harambe, the silverback gorilla that was put down in order to save the life of the child who fell into the exhibit, because it was hurtful to their staff. Nevertheless, the Zoo's call for self-restraint only ignited the mob further, which in turn overwhelmed their social media feed with even more posts and memes involving images and mentions of Harambe. As a result, the Zoo deactivated its Twitter account to escape the disquiet.[4]

A concern present in all of these cases is that the voices in favor of more respectful public dialogue on social media may tend to spiral into silence for fear of being mobbed.[5] As such, social media outlets should consider more carefully how they want to define and enforce community standards for their own platform. In the Leslie Jones case, Twitter eventually banned the mob leader from using its service. But that is just one high-profile incident. More generally across social media platforms, action against mobbing occurs on a case-by-case basis. At the very least, the application of policies seems inconsistent, and it is usually up to the target of offensive posts to initiate the complaint.

In some cases an organized social justice group can help balance out the discourse, such as when @BlackLivesCincy and @theIRATE8 quickly mobilized on social media under the hashtags #SamDuBose and #JusticeForSamDuBose to challenge the framing of DuBose's shooting as justified and were able to help balance public understanding about the meaning and implications of the slaying (see The Irate 8's website, which includes a timeline of events).

Brittany Bibb, one of the founders of the Irate 8, said that initially the group "was never meant to be an organization," but was instead "responding to how people reacted" in the aftermath of the DuBose shooting.[6] Most notably, in its tweets and other social media posts about DuBose, the Irate 8 invoked the #HottestCollegeInAmerica hashtag that was part of the University of Cincinnati's branding and marketing campaign at the time. "We hijacked the #HottestCollegeInAmerica as the first thing we ever did," Bibb said.[7] The #HottestCollegeInAmerica hashtag was popularized by its social media–savvy president at the time, Dr. Santa Ono, and was used by the university's athletics programs, student program, academic units, and others on campus to promote their individual successes by getting into the trending Twitter stream.

At first, the Irate 8 did not even have a Twitter account and relied on individual members coordinating posts through their personal accounts. Instead, #theIrate8 was primarily a hashtag, and its users used it together with the #HottestCollegeInAmerica hashtag in a single post, as a strategy to get hits for their messages within the more popular Twitter stream that #HottestCollegeInAmerica provided. "The hijacking of #HottestCollegeInAmerica was definitely on purpose," said Bibb, who noted that the group often tagged UC President Ono in some of their tweets too. Bibb added: "using that hashtag [#HottestCollegeInAmerica] . . . wherever you look, if you're looking for this famous college president and his social media presence, you're going to find us."[8] Later, the Irate 8 did create its own Twitter account, Bibb explained, to better coordinate group members to like, make comments, and retweet specific posts to get more engagements on Twitter.[9]

However, when there appears to be no mobilized social justice effort, the results can be far different. For instance, there was an uneven display of empathy on social media toward Black and white parents of children involved in tragic incidents during family outings in 2016. A Black family was visiting the Cincinnati Zoo on May 28, 2016, when their three-year-old son climbed over a barrier and fell into a gorilla exhibit, encountering a 450-pound silverback named Harambe. Despite being dragged around, the child was not seriously injured, as zoo staff shot and killed the gorilla within minutes.[10]

Afterwards, the child's mother was widely vilified in a barrage of memes and tweets tagged #JusticeForHarambe for not responsibly looking after her child.[11] An online petition quickly collected a half-million signatures asking that the mother "be held accountable for her lack of supervision and negligence" and further requested a criminal investigation as to whether this was "reflective of the child's home situation." There was widespread outrage that a gorilla was killed due to an "idiot mom" and speculation that she was "shopping for lawyers and celebrating her good fortune." One of the more popular memes pictured Harambe with the caption: "Why did they shoot me? I was doing a better job watching that lady's kid than she was." Rallying under the #JusticeForHarambe hashtag a stream of social media posts seemed to mock the slogans invoked in recent social justice movements after Black males were slain by white police officers (e.g., #JusticeForSamDebose, #Justice4Dontre, #JusticeForTamirRice, and #JusticeForJohnCrawford).

In contrast, similar incidents involving white families did not provoke the same kind of vitriol on social media. In one instance, tagged #DisneyGatorAttack, a two-year-old boy was killed by an alligator at a Disney resort while he splashed around by himself in a shallow lagoon a short distance away from his parents.[12]

There are some important distinctions (besides race) that would account for the more tempered reactions on social media in the latter case. The young child could not be saved, and the parents were suffering unimaginable anguish. Also, the Disney gator attack happened just days after the deadliest mass shooting in U.S. history at the time, which dominated the national news cycle, as well as social media activity.[13]

Another accident happened at the Cleveland Zoo in 2015 when a white mother dropped her child while dangling him over a cheetah exhibit.[14] The boy suffered a broken leg and the mother received probation as a result of the incident. However, there was no widespread campaign on social media to further humiliate the mother, which is in stark contrast to what happened to the Black mother at the Cincinnati Zoo.

While it may be difficult to quantify the disparity in social media reactions between these cases, it is not impossible to see the difference. Whether intentional or not, posters often seem to jump to conclusions based on minimal information contained in a meme or tweet and may further perpetuate insidious forms of racism with hasty likes, shares, and retweets.

While trolls and mean tweets certainly add to the quantity of dialogue taking place on social media, we may at the same time question the quality of this form of public discourse. Ideally, in a society that values free expression, online networks should be a platform for opposing thoughts and viewpoints in a digital marketplace of ideas, without devolving to the communicative equivalent of throwing rocks at each other. Rather, as Brett Johnson has suggested, "digital communication intermediaries like Facebook or Twitter should publish community standards that commit to protecting freedom of expression on their platforms in all but a few clear exceptions," such as threats of violence, pornography, or other criminal content.[15] Too often, online hecklers do not face their opponents, person-to-person, but manage to silence them through threats and intimidation. They can be online mobs "who petition Facebook to remove speech with which they disagree" or take to Twitter and other outlets "to intimidate others who speak up for a cause."[16]

The value of social media as a potential tool for public discourse is that individuals and groups can send their message to a large number of other individuals and groups that are both intended (and not intended) to receive the message, thus contributing to the marketplace of ideas. Addressing this point, Johnson warns that information intermediaries have to be careful to not "allow norm policing and trolling to be amplified to such an extent that it chills potentially valuable speech."[17]

There is already evidence that a small amount of the content online is receiving a large amount of attention. On the internet, audience "attention is clustered around a select few content options, followed by a long tail, in which the remaining multitude of content options each attract very small audiences that in the aggregate can exceed the audience for the 'hits.'"[18] As Johnson explained, "this difference in scale is problematic for public discourse," as the further one's speech is down the long tail, the smaller the marketplace for one's ideas.[19]

Given the rise of Twitter trolls and the ability of some groups to shout down other more reasoned voices in sensitive questions about race, we might also question who is driving traditional political conversations, especially during election cycles. We examine this particular issue using Twitter activity during the U.S. presidential election cycle in 2016, which was also a high point for Twitter-trolling and cyber-bullying in the Harambe and Leslie Jones cases discussed previously. We also wonder what groups, other than social justice advocates, might employ the hashtag hijacking strategies described by Bibb.

chapter 6

election 2016

Trolling in the Twittersphere and Gaming the system

Editor's note: The QR code below will take you to Chapter 6 of the freely available online edition of this book. The online edition differs from the print edition in two major ways. First, the content is written for an audience of scholars and sometimes discusses methodology in greater detail that may not be useful for most readers. Second, the online edition benefits from having the ability to host colorful and interactive images that are not possible to recreate in print. Throughout this chapter the author references detailed figures that represent the information being discussed in the text. By following the link provided by this QR code, you will be able to engage with the cited figures. Because the findings are expertly summarized in this edition, you will not be at risk of missing any of the analysis by not looking at the cited figures. However, some readers may find it helpful to see the data visualized and be able to engage directly with the relevant data sets. Figure references are consistent between both the print and online editions.

https://bit.ly/3Br3MKl

In previous chapters we studied social justice networks and affective publics from the bottom up. The interviews in chapters 4 and 5 provided further insights into how social justice activists engage social media as part of their larger public presentation, as well as specific strategies such as hashtag hijacking. Now, we look at "gaming" the social media networks for political ends. Our case study is the 2016 presidential election in the U.S., where we visualize the structure of Twitter networks from political hashtags across the ideological spectrum (e.g., #MAGA, #ImWithHer, and #FeelTheBern). We look at network structures across the political spectrum and examine how different political strategies might lead to different network structures. Moreover, we look at the extent to which trolls and bots might influence these Twitter networks, as well as the impact that individual Twitter posters had during critical moments of the campaign, especially during the presidential debates between candidates Donald Trump and Hillary Clinton. A related purpose of this set of data visualizations of Twitter activity is to measure the relative popularity of tweets from Russian-based trolls and bots compared to those made by the candidates, celebrities, and other social media influencers. For instance, a Pew Research Center study predicted that it is bots that post about two-thirds of tweeted links to popular websites, rather than humans.[1]

The set of data vitalizations discussed in this chapter were derived from the Twitter historical archive, where we extracted such things as hashtags and words in tweets. We explored tweet-retweet relationships, and produced basic descriptive statistics about the search terms. The nodes (colored circles) that you see in the online data sets consist of Twitter users, and links are built between those users and others who retweeted them. In this process, we preserve important data, such as tweet text and time of tweet, for more detailed exploration, and these are filterable by time, as well as further studies of these data. Our original data can be viewed here: https://themlmom.com/projects/debates.

Looking at the time period around the three presidential debates between candidates Trump and Clinton, pro-Trump tweets tend to have a stronger interrelationship with one another, most notably due to use of the popular #MAGA hashtag. That is, pro-Trump tweets were more likely to be retweeted, or otherwise engaged with by other users. While the pro-Clinton tweets were actually greater in number than the pro-Trump tweets, they were more widely dispersed in the network and had fewer interactions with other users in the network. In some sense this is analogous to the election results, in which Clinton wins the popular vote but loses in the Electoral College based on how votes amass within individual states. While the number of pro-Trump tweets were fewer than the pro-Clinton ones, they were arguably a more impactful force, and are more noticeable in their conglomeration on Twitter. Compared to pro-Clinton tweets, pro-Trump tweets were more cohesive, and were clearly more engaging for users, as they created immense nodes on the network. Ironically, this is in contrast to Clinton's campaign message of "Stronger Together." In terms of Twitter activity, pro-Clinton tweets were scattered apart with fewer engagements overall. Examining Twitter activity this way shows us something that traditional polling failed to predict in the election outcome. At the very least, Twitter visualizations are another way to make sense of the election in ways that the polls did not.

Based on this initial analysis of the data, we wanted to find out which particular Twitter accounts were the most influential in creating pro-Trump activity on the networks. For instance, was Donald Trump's personal Twitter account the most influential, or that of a particular celebrity, or those produced by Russian-based trolls (e.g., the fake "Jenna Abrams" account with 70,000+ followers that was created by the Internet Research Agency from Russia)? To discover this, we performed a series of "knockout experiments" in which we see the impact of individual accounts by removing them from the group of tweets during a selected time period. This allowed us to examine the impact of a particular account by seeing how its absence changed the amount of activty (number of tweets, retweets, comments, etc.). These "knockout" experiments borrow from genetic theory about what happens when you "knock out" genetic code within a DNA sequence to test the impact that a particular code piece has on the entire sequence. To our knowledge, this has not been done in social network analysis before, except on small scales and using broad theories.

Additionally, we wanted to examine "broker figures," which are Twitter accounts that do not necessarily provide new content but provide bridges in the social network through their retweets and number of followers. According to basic social networking theory,[2] if you take out the bridges, you diminish the network. For example, three bot-generated tweets appear to be essential to a large group of pro-Trump tweets (see Figure 1 online via the QR code at the beginning of the chapter). These three tweets each feature Cyrillic scripts, as well as the #Ukraine hashtag.. Other examples are references to the iPhone 7 release in tweets linked to pro-Trump posts, thereby connecting unrelated tweets about the release of a popular mobile device to pro-Trump discourse (see Figure 6.2 online via the QR code at the beginning of the chapter). It appears that bots were gaming the system (or hijacking hashtags) by utilizing some of the most popular (although unrelated) hashtags to increase the exposure of pro-Trump messages, which is a subtle and insidious form of influence. Beyond election messaging, this use of bots challenges the utopian view of social media and social networks, as large nodes can be artificially manufactured with insidious actors trying to game the system.

You can perform your own "knockout" experiments at this link, https://themlmom.com/projects/debates, and observe the growth of several subnetworks, which appear to be right-wing influencers that are not part of the Trump campaign. In essence, the subnetworks of pro-Trump nodes have metastasized and become a highly resilient network overall. Even if you take out the center node, the one from the Trump campaign, the broader network is still there. Some of the most prominent of these subnetworks are nodes formed by the "bfrazer747" node, the "TeamTrump" node, and the "USA4Trump" node (Figure 6.3, 6.4, and 6.5, respectively, online via the QR code at the beginning of the chapter).

Furthermore, even the Twitter accounts of well-established legacy news outlets do not have the same kind of scope of network. See, for instance at the link provided above, ABC's node, CNN's node, and

MSNBC's node (see Figure 6.6, 6.7, and 6.8, respectively, online via QR code at the beginning of the chapter). This shows that mainstream news outlets did not have the same level of influence during this time period as bot-generated accounts or other pro-Trump accounts outside of the campaign. However, this does not necessarily mean that all (or even most) pro-Trump activity on Twitter was fake. It does suggest that pro-Trump accounts were much more effective in working with each other as a network, as opposed to pro-Clinton accounts, which were more isolated from one another. It also indicates that more neutral accounts (represented as mainstream news outlets) were also not as effective in bridging together various groups or as influential in spreading narratives about the campaigns as were pro-Trump actors.

For instance, if you look at the network that surrounds Hillary Clinton's account, the pro-Trump subnetworks have overwhelmed that landscape too. These "subnetworks" consist of a smaller (but not "small") group of pro-Trump accounts. While Trump's Twitter account has all of these subnetworks budding off of him, not all of them are leading back to him. Rather, the pro-Trump subnetworks appear to have their own core of influence, and have even co-opted opposing hashtags, such as "#ImWithHer." This means that pro-Trump accounts were more actively engaged in Twitter activity about Clinton than were pro-Clinton accounts. In summary, the pro-Trump dominance on Twitter is multi-tiered and even legacy media outlets are neutralized in their scope.

Gaming the 2016 Twittersphere: a closer look

Based on the research previously presented, we sought to explore how politically right-leaning entities appear to be more effective at using Twitter to promote their political inclinations and presidential candidate. The previous results (see Figures 6.1–6.8 online via the QR code at the beginning of the chapter) might indicate that this is the result of troll activity, especially how pro-Trump Twitter accounts overwhelmed the node around Hillary Clinton. However, this is still only an assumption about the power of trolls and bots in monopolizing and manipulating the Twittersphere in support of candidate Trump during the 2016 election.

Our subsequent analysis presented below is based on data visualization methods that stemmed from questions about the influence of troll-like behavior from real users who are utilizing troll strategies to support their positions (e.g., inclusion of emojis alongside texts, the insertion of random plug-ins regarding unrelated topics, and the use of extreme and aggressive language).

Definition of terms

In this subsequent analysis we use the term "right-leaning" or "the right" to categorize Twitter handles supportive of candidate Trump, as well as handles expressing anti-Hillary Clinton, anti-Democratic Party, or anti-Obama statements. While many express pro-Trump sentiments directly by positively referencing the Twitter handle @realDonaldTrump, others express their support by lambasting Hillary Clinton while simultaneously using "left-leaning" hashtags such as #ImWithHer alongside the use of right-leaning hashtags such as #MAGA.

We use the terms "left-leaning" or "the left" to categorize handles with pro-Hillary Clinton content. More often "the left" is represented by handles strongly opposing Donald Trump.

Methodology

This subsequent study includes a one percent sample of all Twitter data from the date ranges of September 25–27, 2016, and November 6–8, 2016, and examines the data in three ways:

1. We examined the centrality of individual Twitter handles, represented as nodes in the visualization of the network, and measure for statistical significance through numerical data. This would show us which particular Twitter accounts were the most significant, or central, to the network.

2. We also looked at the co-occurrence of the major hashtags during these same two time periods, where tweets from both the left and the right are analyzed to determine the use of hashtag co-occurrence by parties supportive of either side of the debate. That is, we wanted to see which hashtags are most popularly paired with other hashtags in the network. The top 50 hashtags for betweenness and degree are used to determine the frequency of co-occurrence. Numerical graphs as well as bar graphs are used to dictate both the number of hashtags used by each group and the rate at which each utilizes co-occurrence within their network. Combined with the bar graphs, networks of the left and right, as well as the (or pairing a hashtag with other hashtags) within the larger network, where the top eight hashtags are highlighted, provided visual representations of co-occurrence.

3. We also performed a series of "knockout experiments" in which major nodes within the larger network are removed to determine their influence on the broader network. Visuals examine the larger network within September and November and highlight the major nodes essential to the structure and stability of the network. In addition to knockouts, this section includes visuals where major nodes are highlighted to present and compare their places within the network.

Centrality

When looking at the centrality of specific Twitter handles throughout September 25–27, 2016, we found that @realDonaldTrump (the official Twitter account of candidate Trump) was the highest in degree, and @HillaryClinton (the official Twitter account of candidate Clinton) was the second highest (see Figure 6.9 online via the QR code at the beginning of the chapter). While Trump's Twitter account outperformed Clinton's in its significance in the overall network, our findings also showed that each of the candidate's accounts were central to their own network of supporters on Twitter.

A majority of the handles that are highest in degree are pro-right handles (i.e., realDonaldTrump, DanScavino, LindaSuhler, bfraser747, magnifier661, TeamTrump, CarmineZozzara, The_Trump_Train, and StatesPoll). These major nodes hover around the two candidates as the first debate on September 26, 2016, unfolds. These major handles attract the most Twitter volume and draw the most attention to the debates surrounding their favored candidate, Donald Trump.

Donald Trump's official Twitter account, @realDonaldTrump, also rates highest in connecting other users with the network together, while Hillary Clinton's account, @HillaryClinton, places second. As illustrated in Figure 6.10 (see online via the QR code at the beginning of the chapter), the other top handles in linking various users together are mostly supporters of the right. This showcases the strength of the right within the network and their role as an integral part in connecting others to the network. Some of the same handles highest in degree resurface as highest in betweenness. You may also recognize that some of the same handles rated highest in centrality (see Figure 6.9 online via the QR code at the beginning of the chapter) resurface as highest in Figure 6.10. Again, most of those reoccurring handles are supportive of Trump and the right.

Also telling is the use of hashtags by the candidates during the September 25–27, 2016, time period around the first presidential debate. In Figure 6.11 (via the QR code at the beginning of the chapter), we can see that the #MAGA hashtag is the most dominant. However, @HillaryClinton does not use any hashtags in her posts, except #LoveTrumpsHate, and only once during the days encompassing this first debate.

Moreover, in a closer examination of Figure 6.11 (see online via the QR code at the beginning of the chapter) we can see that the @HillaryClinton account does not use recognizable or popular hashtags. Rather, activity around that account it is dominated by various pro-right accounts. Therefore, we might infer that the @HillaryClinton handle maintains its high ranking (second within the network) due to the many right-leaning handles who use her handle as a mechanism to attract users to their own pro-Trump views. At the same time, however, @realDonaldTrump utilizes the #MAGA hashtag in several of his posts, as well as #MakeAmericaGreatAgain and #TrumpTrain. Many of the other pro-right handles employ these same hashtags in their own tweets—and alongside several left-leaning hashtags, which seems to be a significant factor in their overall dominance of the network.

Now let us look at the data and visualizations from November 6–8, 2016 (see Figure 6.12 online via the QR code at the beginning of the chapter), which was the three-day period leading up to the election. Again, @realDonaldTrump rates the highest in degree, but the @HillaryClinton account has dropped from second down to third. Moreover, Donald Trump, Jr. (@DonaldTrumpJr), candidate Trump's eldest son, has moved into second place.

Even further, the majority of handles that are highest in degree are pro-right handles, including @realDonaldTrump, @DonaldJTrumpJr, @DanScavino, @LouDobbs, @EricTrump, @LindaSuhler, and @TomiLahren). Similar to the previous period of September 25–27, the major nodes of activity hover around the two candidates, as the major handles attract the most Twitter volume and draw the most attention. The most noticeable difference in the November 6–8 time period, though, is that the second highest account is another Trump supporter, @DonaldJTrumpJr, who had overtaken the other candidate in the race—@HillaryClinton—within the Twittersphere. While there is also a growth of some left-leaning celebrities, such as @ladygaga and @rihanna, they are only seen in the periphery of the network, rather than at the center of the action.

Additionally, two of the handles besides @realDonaldTrump, @DanScavino, and @LindaSuhler are present among the top handles for degree in both the September and November time periods, while @HillaryClinton is the only repeated left-leaning handle in both periods. This may help to explain the strength of the right and their ability to create a more inclusive and stronger network. These handles could be constituted as "loyal followers" since they play a leading role in September, while also maintaining their place within the network for the month of November. This is not the case with the left, whose supportive handles play a less consistent role within the Twitterverse. Although the support for the left within this snapshot seems to become more equitable than it was for September (meaning there are more Twitter handles who are left-leaning among this list), the lack of consistency mentioned above may account for the strength of the right's network, despite the fact that more left-leaning hashtags are coming out to support their candidate. Perhaps they came out too late, or simply did not conform to similar themes and messages to be effective?

Many of the handles are pro-right and vary in their hashtags (discussed later in the section on co-occurrence). Similarly, two of the pro-right handles (besides @realDonaldTrump), @DanScavino and @LindaSuhler, are present in the top handles for betweenness for the September and November periods; and again, @HillaryClinton is the only repeated left-leaning handle. This role of supporting handles is not the case with the left, whose supportive handles play a less consistent role within the Twitterverse during these time periods.

Figures 6.14, 6.15, and 6.16 (see online via the QR code at the beginning of the chapter) show how central Trump is to the overall network, although the various nodes surrounding both candidates are right-leaning handles. In comparison, many on the outskirts are the top left-leaning supporters in terms of degree. @HillaryClinton is still central to the network but is virtually dwarfed by the density of clusters and individual nodes surrounding @realDonaldTrump. Additionally, when comparing these two major handles and their edges, it is clear that more edges stem from @realDonaldTrump compared to those stemming from @HillaryClinton. While @HillaryClinton contains several edges connected to nodes along the periphery, @realDonaldTrump is much more connected to other nodes, where their connections through distinct edges are prominent. These visualizations indicate that candidate Trump's account was a more integral bridge actor within the Twitter network, meaning that more groups of supporters on the right were interconnected through interaction with his account (via likes, retweets, etc.). On the other hand, candidate Clinton's account was less effective in bridging together various left-leaning users. Trump and the right were a more congealed force on Twitter.

Co-occurrence of hashtags

We took the top 50 handles in betweenness from the time period September 25–27, 2016, to address the co-occurrence between hashtags. Across the top and down the left side are the nine most popular hashtags. Each box includes the number of times the hashtag along the left side is paired with the hashtag across the top. From left to right diagonally going down are the total number of hashtags within this network (see Figure 6.17).

	MAGA	ImWithHer	Never Hillary	MakeAmerica GreatAgain	Never Trump	Trump Train	Trump Pence 16	America First	Debate 2016
MAGA	26/26	2/5	8/12	6/6	1/2	7/7	8/8	3/3	4/5
ImWithHer	2/26	5/5	0/12	0/6	0/2	2/7	0/8	0/3	0/5
NeverHillary	8/26	0/5	12/12	2/6	0/2	2/7	2/8	2/3	3/5
MakeAmericaGreatAgain	6/26	0/5	2/12	6/6	0/2	2/7	2/8	2/3	2/5
NeverTrump	1/26	0/5	0/12	0/6	2/2	0/7	1/8	0/3	0/5
TrumpTrain	7/26	2/5	2/12	2/6	0/2	7/7	1/8	1/3	0/5
TrumpPence16	8/26	0/5	2/12	2/6	1/2	1/7	8/8	2/3	3/5
AmericaFirst	3/26	0/5	2/12	2/6	0/2	1/7	2/8	3/3	2/5
Debate2016	4/26	0/5	3/12	2/6	0/2	0/7	3/8	2/3	5/5

Figure 6.17
Co-occurrence of top hashtags in betweenness

The two most popular hashtags among the top 50 handles include #MAGA and #ImWithHer. #MAGA occurs in 26 of these top 50 handles, whereas #ImWithHer is present in just 5 handles. #NeverHillary also outnumbers #ImWithHer, with 12 hashtags present among these top 50 handles, as does #TrumpTrain with 7 hashtags and #TrumpPence16 with 8 hashtags. Co-occurrence among #MAGA is also much higher than #ImWithHer. While the use of particular hashtags in great numbers might be indicative of support, perhaps, more importantly, it inherently conveys power simply by its usage. When comparing the hashtag #MAGA with #ImWithHer it is clear that #MAGA co-occurs with other hashtags far more than does #ImWithHer. In fact, the only two hashtags that co-occur with #ImWithHer are both right-leaning hashtags (#MAGA and #TrumpTrain). The rest do not co-occur (see Figure 6.18 online via the QR code at the beginning of the chapter).

	MAGA	ImWithHer	Never Hillary	MakeAmerica GreatAgain	Never Trump	Trump Train	Trump Pence 16	America First	Debate 2016	Average
MAGA		0.40	0.67	1.00	0.50	1.00	1.00	1.00	0.80	0.80
ImWithHer	0.08		0.00	0.00	0.00	0.29	0.00	0.00	0.00	0.05
NeverHillary	0.31	0.00		0.33	0.00	0.29	0.25	0.67	0.60	0.31
MakeAmericaGreatAgain	0.23	0.00	0.17		0.00	0.29	0.25	0.67	0.40	0.25
NeverTrump	0.04	0.00	0.00	0.00		0.00	0.13	0.00	0.00	0.02
TrumpTrain	0.27	0.40	0.17	0.33	0.00		0.13	0.33	0.00	0.20
TrumpPence16	0.31	0.00	0.17	0.33	0.50	0.14		0.67	0.60	0.34
AmericaFirst	0.12	0.00	0.17	0.33	0.00	0.14	0.25		0.40	0.18
Debate2016	0.15	0.00	0.25	0.33	0.00	0.00	0.38	0.67		0.22
Average	0.19	0.10	0.20	0.33	0.13	0.27	0.30	0.50	0.35	0.26
	1.50	0.80	1.58	2.67	1.00	2.14	2.38	4.00	2.80	

Figure 6.18

Percentage chart for co-occurrence: September 25–27, 2016

Figure 6.19 (see online via the QR code at the beginning of the chapter) highlights the comparisons between co-occurrence from the left and the right. As the bar graph shows, Trump supporters, or those representing the right, are more likely to layer their hashtags. For instance, the term MAGA ranks highest in terms of co-occurrence. Each color represents a hashtag paired with each one of the other hashtags. The amount of color visible among representations of each hashtag signifies the percentage of co-occurrence between these two hashtags. For instance, #MAGA is sixth in comparison to other right-supporting / Trump-supporting hashtags, such as #NeverHillary and #MakeAmericaGreatAgain; the left-supporting hashtags, #ImWithHer and #NeverTrump, experience very little co-occurrence. Additionally, #NeverTrump is accompanied by only Trump-supportive hashtags #MAGA and #TrumpPence16. Most notably, #MAGA is the most popular of the hashtags and is paired with the most other hashtags, including neutral ones like #Debate2016, and has a multiplier effect by using combinations of hashtags for one tweet.

Figure 6.20 identifies #MAGA as the prominent hashtag used among the top 50 handles in degree, among the 32 hashtags present in this instance. Again, the top used was #MAGA, followed by #NeverHillary (second), #TrumpTrain (third), #TrumpPence2016 (fourth), and then #MakeAmericaGreatAgain (fifth). All of these top handles are right-leaning and do a much better job of co-occurring with one another.

	MAGA	ImWithHer	Never Hillary	MakeAmerica GreatAgain	Never Trump	Trump Train	Trump Pence 16	America First	Debate 2016
MAGA	32/32	1/6	11/13	8/9	1/4	12/12	10/10	5/5	5/6
ImWithHer	1/32	6/6	0/13	0/9	2/4	1/12	0/10	0/5	1/6
NeverHillary	11/32	0/6	13/13	2/9	0/4	3/12	4/10	3/5	3/6
MakeAmericaGreatAgain	8/32	0/6	2/13	9/9	0/4	2/12	2/10	2/5	2/6
NeverTrump	1/32	2/6	0/13	0/9	4/4	0/12	1/10	0/5	1/6
TrumpTrain	12/32	1/6	3/13	2/9	0/4	12/12	4/10	2/5	0/6
TrumpPence16	10/32	0/6	4/13	2/9	1/4	4/12	10/10	4/5	3/6
AmericaFirst	5/32	0/6	3/13	2/9	0/4	2/12	4/10	5/5	2/6
Debate2016	5/32	1/6	3/13	2/9	1/4	0/12	3/10	2/5	6/6

Figure 6.20
Top 50 in degree, September 25–27

To measure highest in degree between September 26–27, 2016, we took the top 50 Twitter handles and looked at the co-occurrence between these hashtags. In Figure 6.21, across the top and down the left side are the nine hashtags, which note the highest in popularity. Each box includes the number of times the hashtag along the left side is paired with the hashtag across the top. The #MAGA hashtag dominates, towering over the rest with 32 uses; it is frequently paired with #NeverHillary, and again has a multiplier effect by using combinations of hashtags for just one tweet. Additionally, the neutral hashtag #Debate2016 is paired with #MAGA five out of six times, whereas it is only paired with the pro-Hillary hashtag, #ImWithHer, one of six times. The right is much better at grouping using neutral hashtags.

	MAGA	ImWithHer	Never Hillary	MakeAmerica GreatAgain	Never Trump	Trump Train	Trump Pence 16	America First	Debate 2016	Average
MAGA		0.17	0.85	0.89	0.25	1.00	1.00	1.00	0.83	0.75
ImWithHer	0.03		0.00	0.00	0.50	0.08	0.00	0.00	0.17	0.10
NeverHillary	0.34	0.00		0.22	0.00	0.25	0.40	0.60	0.50	0.29
MakeAmericaGreatAgain	0.25	0.00	0.15		0.00	0.17	0.20	0.40	0.33	0.19
NeverTrump	0.03	0.33	0.00	0.00		0.00	0.10	0.00	0.17	0.08
TrumpTrain	0.38	0.17	0.23	0.22	0.00		0.40	0.40	0.00	0.22
TrumpPence16	0.31	0.00	0.31	0.22	0.25	0.33		0.80	0.50	0.34
AmericaFirst	0.16	0.00	0.23	0.22	0.00	0.17	0.40		0.33	0.19
Debate2016	0.16	0.17	0.23	0.22	0.25	0.00	0.30	0.40		0.22
Average	0.21	0.10	0.25	0.25	0.16	0.25	0.35	0.45	0.35	0.26
	1.66	0.83	2.00	2.00	1.25	2.00	2.80	3.60	2.83	

Figure 6.21

Percentage chart for highest in-betweenness

Additionally, the right has more overlap in its use of hashtags in comparison to the left and there are fewer hashtags to compare between pro-left hashtag users. This shows that the right used more hashtags than the left overall and used more hashtags together within a single tweet.

While some of the left-leaning hashtags that are present in the network we're employed by more popular accounts (often belonging to pro-Trump supporters and connected to pro-Trump hashtags), there is some interconnection among the more popular of the pro-Clinton accounts and other followers among the left (see Figure 6.23 online via the QR code at the beginning of the chapter for more details). However, within the broader Twitterverse, pro-Clinton activities are only sparsely connected, especially when compared to the pro-Trump activity on the network.

When looking at the right-leaning hashtags (see Figure 6.24 online via the QR code at the beginning of the chapter) a much more interconnected network is visible, as the activity appears deeply intertwined with different communities on Twitter and among individual users. Moreover, the major hubs of activity connected to specific users are closely related (through bridge actors) to other popular centers of action. Interestingly, pro-Trump hashtags were notably paired with a singular, more neural hashtag, #ElectionDay. This is very different from the left, since their hashtags are much more diverse, even around the major hubs of activity. Rather than only attracting handles or followers using the same hashtag, these major centers of activity on the right are able to attract more users who are using various other hashtags. This also reflects the success of co-occurrence used by top handles, since the major nodes are attracting followers that use various hashtags within their post as opposed to followers using the same hashtags.

When comparing Figures 6.23 and 6.24 (see online via the QR code at the beginning of the chapter), it is evident that while the left is more diverse in its use of hashtags that occupy its major nodes, the right's consistent use of the #ElectionDay hashtag, as well as its pairing of other hashtags, contributed to its dominance of the network that day. The left appeared to have less interaction (or communication) among its users on the network that day, as well as less usage of hashtags or paired hashtags linking similar (or disparate) themes and messages. In contrast, there is much more communication occurring between the right notes, where multiple hashtags are associated with each of the major hubs of activity on the right. Again, this is an dictation that both the handles following these major nodes and the major nodes themselves are successful in pairing hashtags and therefore attracting followers using multiple hashtags, sometimes even many at the same time.

Knockout experiments

When looking at Figures 6.25 and 6.26 (see online via the QR code at the beginning of the chapter), there appears to be little change when the

@realDonaldTrump handle is removed from the network. Outside of the individual nodes once surrounding the @realDonaldTrump handle, many of the major connections appear to remain within the network. The edge networks also appear to remain intact, as the less significant handles and the edge networks are connected to other major nodes within the network.

Similar to the removal of @realDonaldTrump the removal of @HillaryClinton (see Figure 6.27 online via the QR code at the beginning of the chapter) does little to disturb the network. While those hovering around this former node have dispersed, their connections to other major nodes have allowed these less significant nodes to maintain their space within the overall network. Furthermore, the rest of the network remains unscathed by the removal of @HillaryClinton from the network. While this may seem to suggest that the @HillaryClinton Twitter handle is unimportant within the network, @realDonaldTrump's equally lackluster impact on the network after its removal suggests the importance of other major nodes/handles within the network and their ability to sustain support for their prospective candidates despite their candidates' absence from the network. This suggests that candidate Trump has an active and more interconnected core of supporters on Twitter that Clinton lacked.

Even without several of the major nodes (see Figure 6.28 online via the QR code at the beginning of the chapter), the right's network remains visibly intact. While the candidates' Twitter accounts, @realDonaldTrump and @HillaryClinton, have some influence on the network, they are not the only major nodes keeping the network together. This suggests that strong political networks are made up of several independent nodes that not only support their preferred candidate, but that also build a fan base (or community) around themselves. These make for a stronger network, where the major node, @realDonaldTrump, is not necessarily essential for the stability of the network.

When looking at Figure 6.29 (see online via the QR code at the beginning of the chapter), many of the major nodes on the right (@EricTrump, @TeamTrump, @LouDobbs, @LindaSuhler, @rudygiulianiGOP,

@WDFx2EU8) are removed along with @realDonaldTrump. Here the overall network is visibly starting to collapse. Nonetheless, even with @realDonaldTrump gone and with many of his top followers on the right removed, the network is able to exist and still contains many Trump-supportive hashtags.

Figure 6.30 (see online via the QR code at the beginning of the chapter) shows the major Twitter nodes supporting the right among the top 25 hashtags in degree. These nodes are highest in degree in the larger network, as well as in their connection to other parts of the network. Highlighted hashtags include only those supportive of the right. These nodes, or Twitter handles, include @DonaldJTrumpJr, @DanScavino, @LouDobbs, @EricTrump, @LindaSuhler, @TomiLahren, @TeamTrump, @rudygiulianiGOP, @Lrihendry, @WDFx2EU8 (which may be a handle belonging to a bot, or troll), @WeNeedTrump, @ChristiChat, @bfraser747, @mike_pence, @Stonewall_77, and @LaraLeaTrump. In comparison to the left-leaning handles, these nodes form a clear circle around the two major candidates and can be seen actively participating in connections not only between these major candidates and other supportive nodes, but also interacting with and connecting to one another, helping to form a circle, or rather star-like shape, encircling the candidates' nodes (@realDonaldTrump and @HillaryClinton).

Comparing this to the major left-leaning nodes highest in degree (see Figure 6.31 online via the QR code at the beginning of the chapter), the right-leaning handles within the network almost resemble an attacking force surrounding the two major candidates. It also seems like some of the major left-leaning supporters (again, mostly celebrities) fall outside the periphery of the graph, as discussed below.

In Figure 6.31 (see online via the QR code at the beginning of the chapter), the following handles are highlighted: @rihanna, @ladygaga, @NormaniKordei, @ChrisEvans, @ddlovato, @JLo, and @thatbloodyMikey. It is clear that many of these nodes outside of @ladygaga (in the upper left corner) and @ddlovato (the one highlighted edge from the upper righthand corner) do not have a strong connection to the network. Many of these left handles consist of celebrities and are found along the periphery. In fact, outside of the two handles mentioned, many of these handles cannot be seen. It also seems as if they are attached more strongly and centrally to @realDonaldTrump, rather than @HillaryClinton, despite the fact that they are more supportive of candidate Hillary Clinton and use hashtags supportive of her. This indicates a lack of bridging and a weaker (or more dispersed) network in spite of the number of individuals supporting Clinton on the overall network.

In comparison to the right-leaning hashtags, these nodes are far removed from the conversation, figuratively and literally. There is not only disconnect from the main participants in the network, but there also appears to be little conversation occurring between these major nodes. This speaks to the lack of left-leaning nodes among the top 25, but also addresses the inability of these nodes to speak to the larger issues and more popular hashtags promulgated throughout the network.

Major Findings

From the data presented here, the right is far better at gaining attention and traction within the network via hashtags, as demonstrated in the visuals and numerical value attributed to the betweenness and centrality of right-leaning hashtags. Meanwhile, bots and major news outlets are not prominent within the network, as the majority of the top-ranking handles (as dictated by betweenness and degree) are prominent Twitter users, such as politicians, or others with ties to the presidential race, including celebrities (especially during the November 6–8, 2016, range).

The right does a much better job of pairing hashtags alongside one another within their tweets. This is a product of the right using more hashtags, and also because the prominent hashtags in the network consist predominantly of right-leaning hashtags. Additionally, the right in several cases links left-leaning hashtags, such as #ImWithHer alongside #MAGA, in ways that promote their candidate of choice, while deriding his opponent.

While the handle @realDonaldTrump is a major figure within the network, the figures presented here, as well as the knockout experiments, show the strength of the right within the network even when their protagonist, Trump, is completely absent from the network. This is indicative of the strength of the right's Twitter network. In fact, there was no major node that, when removed, was able to dismantle the network alone. It would take the removal of several of these major nodes for any distinguishable changes to occur.

That said, given the prominence of fake news sources that employed bots during the election campaign cycle of 2016, we might question what impact they had. While the right demonstrates a strong Twitter network in and of itself, we now consider the more difficult-to-measure impact of fake news, bots, and doublespeak on the Twitterverse throughout 2016, and lessons social justice movements might take from the right in their use of social networking applications.

However, a limitation of our analyses of the Twitter data sets in this section was our focus on hashtags instead of specific conversations. As we have noted in previous chapters, tweets that contain powerful images or resonant emotions can go viral without the use of hashtags. To be clear, we are not suggesting here that right-leaning networks are more cohesive based on the resonance of particular messages; rather, our analyses do show how virality can be manipulated through the use of hashtags. There is of course real power in other kinds of tweets (without exploiting hashtags) that have power in their own right and may ultimately affect social discourse on social media platforms. In the next chapter we take a deeper look at the political and commercial manipulation of social media discourse, as well as its input on news, information, and technology.

chapter 7

Fake News, Bots, and Doublespeak

While our previous chapter focused on political discourses, the internet, and mobile telecommunications, social media platforms have also become integral to our social lives and how we get news and information. A Pew Research study showed that 67 percent of Americans get news from social media, which is up 62 percent from the year before.[1] This presents not only a challenge for the institution of journalism but also a crisis in how our society discerns information and truth in public discourse. Knowing the difference between real and fake news, as well as truth and misinformation, has become increasingly problematic with the proliferation of tweets, memes, and so-called alternative facts. With open platforms on social media, anyone can share practically anything with everyone without any fact-checking filters, making it difficult to separate credible sources of information from specious ones.

Moreover, "bots" allow users to automate hundreds of posts from a single social media account within a day and spread false information from fake news sites at levels that can make it appear legitimate. "Bots" is short for "robots"; these are automated software programs that operate on social media platforms. They perform specific tasks, such as making posts, giving the appearance of representing a real person interacting and engaging on social media. For instance, two of the most popular conservative Twitter pundits during the 2016 presidential election campaign, "Jenna Abrams" and "Pamela Moore," were eventually found out to be

Russian trolls, manufactured by the now infamous Internet Research Agency. The "Jenna Abrams" account had over 70,000 followers, and combined with others from the same farm had immeasurable reach, if not effect, as bots can give the illusion of viral popularity for particular political perspectives and candidates.

Although bot-generated messages do not exercise mind control over social media users, when cranked out by the thousands upon thousands, they do allow certain ideological frames about timely political issues and candidates to gain saliency over others (e.g., "crooked Hillary," "lock her up," "build the wall," "liberal media," "Pizzagate", etc.). Bot-generated tweets and ads posted on Facebook or Instagram from a broad array of accounts—"Jenna Abrams," "Pamela Moore," "Army of Jesus," "Heart of Texas," and many others—provide their own digital echo chamber and manufacture the prevalence of a certain kind of thinking, including thinking about issues related to elections as well as social justice.

The exploitation of fake news on social media became a point of controversy in the 2016 U.S. presidential election cycle after reports about Russians micro-targeting key voting districts in Ohio, as well as in Wisconsin, Michigan, and Pennsylvania, with fake news stories on Facebook. Whether or not there was political intent to sway voters' opinions, there was nonetheless a commercial incentive to produce stories with salacious headlines that would cater to individual biases, and more importantly, draw "clicks."[2]

Bloomberg News reported that an engineering manager at Twitter discovered a hoard of Russian and Ukrainian spam accounts in 2015, but the company did not delete them because doing so could be interpreted as a decline in popularity of the social media network. In Congressional testimony, the estimated number of fake accounts from Russia was reported to be over 36,000. For its part, Facebook estimates that at least 146 million of its users were exposed to advertisements purchased as part of a Russian campaign.[3] Again, it is difficult to directly quantify the impact of those ads, but it does point to a more significant problem presented by a culture that, perhaps, is losing its ability to recognize and appreciate epistemic rigor.

Epistemology refers to an understanding of how we know things. For instance, science, and the scientific method, is one of the most regimented ways of knowing, as it produces empirical knowledge that is based upon direct and measured observation of specified phenomena. University professors and investigative journalists can be recognized as members of epistemic communities, as they employ empiricism in the discovery of knowledge and truth. The problem presented by fake news and misinformation is that it presents a sophistic kind of epistemology in which knowledge is based on what one wants to believe and is merely rooted in clever tweets and memes. As described by Plato, sophists used crafty rhetoric to make logically flawed arguments persuasive. Today we see sophistry as a form of post-truth discourse, where biases shape all news and information, and thus one source is no more or less valid than any other. No matter what the actual truth may be, there are "alternative facts" that offer another explanation consistent with one's own worldview or self-interest.

George Orwell is credited for presenting the concept of "doublespeak" in his novel 1984, about a dystopian society in which "Big Brother," the leader of the ruling party of a totalitarian state, uses what is termed "doublethink" to present patently hypocritical ideas as normal: "war is peace," "freedom is slavery," and "ignorance is strength."[4] Orwell also coined the term "newspeak" as an ideological form of language that ultimately leads to unclear reasoning. Although Orwell never used the term "doublespeak," it has become fashionable to merge his concepts of "doublethink" and "newspeak" into a single term—"doublespeak"— referring to a form of rhetorical deception.

President Donald Trump regularly engaged in his own brand of doublespeak when describing any reporting about his administration that happens to be unfavorable as "fake news," in addition to his denigrating attacks on journalists and journalism. From the campaign trail to the Oval Office, Trump stoked hatred and distrust of legacy news media by frequently describing the press and reporters as "dishonest," "scum," "horrible people," "sleaze," and "the enemy of the people." These slurs are particularly troubling as they put actual fake news on an equal platform with journalistic institutions. In Trumpian doublespeak the real news is fake.

During Congressional hearings about fake news on social media, some started looking to the law to address the problem. However, the First Amendment provides a broad right of free expression, except in very rare circumstances such as blackmail, fraud, incitement, and child pornography. Moreover, most fake news or misinformation is likely to be regarded as "political speech," which is at the heart of what the First Amendment is supposed to protect. Rather than trying to regulate false speech, it has been fashionable in U.S. jurisprudence to apply the "marketplace of ideas" metaphor, and trust in the self-righting process. Supreme Court Justice Louis Brandeis said that the way to counter falsehood, fallacies, and lies is with more speech—speech that is true.

However, fake news and Trumpian doublespeak may have exposed a fatal flaw in the marketplace-of-ideas metaphor, as the truth doesn't necessarily emerge in a bot-generated barrage of sophistic tweets, posts, and memes. Moreover, Brandeis asserted that the news media is key to fostering an educated and well-informed public to make the marketplace of ideas work. In the post-truth world, though, the institution of journalism is the central target of doublespeak and its status is diminished.

Perhaps a public that values accurate and credible information is needed before journalism can perform its epistemic function. Only educated news audiences, or those motivated by a concern for accuracy, will critically distinguish sources of information, and take responsibility for what they communicate to others, whether it's a share, a like, or a retweet. Only then will journalists be able to reclaim their status as an epistemic community, allowing audiences to consider the meaning of what might otherwise seem to be isolated bits of information. Before we can have an institution that successfully supports the exploration of truth, we need an audience with the critical literacy to appreciate that something can be true based on evidence, even if it is counter to our political worldviews. Otherwise, we will be left to swim through a digital marketplace of commercial and political appeals that will manufacture versions of reality in their own interest.

As the subsequent political economic analysis to be presented as a part of this project will show, the growth and distribution of fake news via bots on social media during the 2016 U.S. presidential cycle, along with doublespeak about what is considered "fake news," has had a detrimental impact on the institutional effectiveness of journalism and has exposed an epistemic flaw in the oft-cited "marketplace of ideas" metaphor used in First Amendment jurisprudence. We will consider the impact on political discourse and social justice efforts.

Social media, social problems, and social justice

Given the political economic limitations of the digital marketplace of ideas described in this chapter, particularly in relation to national politics, questions must be raised about how social media is prone to manipulation around social problems and social justice efforts. Just as fake news played a critical role in the 2016 presidential election, similar concerns are present in the realm of social justice, as the largest Black Lives Matter page on Facebook was found out to be a fake one.[5]

In January 2019 a fake account on Twitter flamed controversy around a Covington, Kentucky, Catholic high school, with a viral video showing students wearing "Make America Great Again" hats while confronting a Native American man in Washington, D.C., on the National Mall. A caption with the post claimed that the students were yelling "build the wall." It turned out that the account that initially posted the video was deactivated because it checked several boxes for being a fake account. Ostensibly, the account belonged to a California teacher, but Twitter determined that it actually originated from Brazil and had an inordinate number of followers (approximately 40,000) for a non-celebrity, similar to the fake "Jenna Abrams" account described earlier.

A different video of the same incident emerged later that provided more details, more context, and further distinction than the original video that went viral. However, this later video came about after national outrage had already focused on the Covington Catholic High School students. Instead of having an informed public discourse about the

event, a single fake Twitter account was able to spark political indigna-
tion over the incident by presenting it within a narrow frame of cultural
politics. Even after the later video emerged, which showed that the
students were not necessarily the sole aggressors in the incident, it was
too little and too late to quell the controversy surrounding the students.

Furthermore, what seemed to bother social justice advocates was
the disparity in how the white youths targeted by trolling after the
initial video were treated with broader empathy after the longer video
emerged—something that would not seem possible for Black people
in somewhat similar situations, such as the Harambe incident in
Cincinnati, which occurred a few years earlier.

Social media is the digital frontline of confrontations, where groups
of people immediately stake out entrenched positions in the immediacy
of a moment—and then vigorously defend that position, rather than
engaging in discourse and moving to potentially changing positions
based on new information, context, and nuance. Social media tends to
present an epistemology of memes, mean tweets, trolling, and bullying,
while legacy news media struggles to catch up and provide the context
and nuance with more information to better understand events taking
place.

In the Covington Catholic incident, it appeared that an entity (outside
of the three that were actually involved) manufactured a version of
reality and stoked emotions in such a way that no one wanted to concede
any ground in their understanding of the event. Even in the aftermath
of the confrontation, spectators on social media seemed closed off to
perspectives and facts that contradicted their original position about
the event. This phenomenon seems distinct in the post-2016 national
cultural political divide. Social media amplifies emotions, especially
fear, anger, and outrage. Those who were originally critical of the Covington Catholic students claimed that legacy reporting of further details
that emerged was an attempt to whitewash the incident and excuse otherwise boorish behavior by the students. Indirectly, it also presented a
challenge to journalistic norms, which are to cover all sides of a story
and provide as much information as possible. This further eroded trust

in news media. In process, the artificial nature of the viral tweet in conjunction with the refutation of additional information about the event in D.C. gives some a means to dismiss legitimate claims of social injustice. Accordingly, the next chapter examines the manipulation of social justice activities on social media, and we will return to the Covington Catholic case in particular to further illuminate some of these points.

chapter 8

The Political Economy of Social Media Networks, Social Justice, and Truth

This chapter brings together an examination of social justice and political discourse in critical political economic perspective, and endeavors to contribute to an ongoing critical-cultural examination of the interplay among online social networks, political economics, and social justice. This includes Christian Fuchs's *Culture and Economy in the Age of Social Media*, which examined critical cultural theory as applied to the culture and economy of social media, and Zizi Papacharissi's "Affective Publics: Sentiment, Technology and Politics," which provided an insightful analysis of the affective nature of Twitter streams within political debates.[1] From our analysis, the political economic struggle that is taking place throughout online networks can be seen as two opposing forces: social justice efforts from the bottom up, and social propaganda from the top down. Other artificially created communities, in which social networks' business models generate links between people, figure into this as well.

We examine the political economy of social media networks by applying Edward Herman and Noam Chomsky's classic propaganda model to the digital marketplace of ideas and find that too often seemingly grassroots movements can be manufactured from the top down via social media networks, confounding social justice movements and confusing epistemic validity within political discourse.[2]

Social media has become an increasingly integral source for how we get news and information. While this may be a good indication about the popularity of social media, it also presents a problem for the institutional effectiveness of journalism in the United States and, more important, for the quality of information within political discourse.

Knowing the difference between real and fake news, as well as truth and falsity, has become increasingly problematic on social media and in this so-called age of post-truth.[3] On open social media platforms anyone can share practically anything with anyone else without any quality or fact-checking filters. As a result, fake news and misinformation distributed through social media can confuse political discourse, making it difficult to discern credible news outlets from specious ones. Moreover, "bots" allow users to automate hundreds of posts from a single social media account within a day and spread false information from fake news sites at levels that make it appear legitimate. Legitimate actors unwittingly share misinformation or engage in public discourse on subjects on which they are insufficiently informed, like what happened with the spread of misinformation about the efficacy of hydroxychloroquine as a treatment for coronavirus during the early stages of the COVID-19 pandemic in 2020, furthers this conundrum.[4]

The political economic analysis presented in this chapter will examine the impact of fake news via social media by applying Edward Herman and Noam Chomsky's famous "propaganda model," which described how ownership, advertising, sourcing, flak, and anti-communism shape media behavior and content.[5] In applying each of these factors to the present social media environment, which can be manipulated through the use of bots and muddled by doublespeak about what is and is not fake news, it appears that the production of fake news may do more than "manufacture consent"; it reconstructs the very perception of truth itself. Accordingly, this analysis further considers the limits of the oft-cited marketplace of ideas metaphor for discerning truth, and addresses the epistemic problem confronting the U.S. institution of journalism and its news audiences.

The political economy of news media: a propaganda model

A political economic analysis of fake news on social media, specifically using Herman and Chomsky's propaganda model, will be a valuable addition to the critical study of how digital technologies have been used to transform journalism. As McChesney described, the political economy of media "is a field that endeavors to connect how media and communication systems and content are shaped by ownership, market structures, commercial support, technologies, labor practices, and government policies."[6] In this sense, political economy can be thought of as a study of media business, but from a decidedly moral and philosophical perspective.[7]

One of the more famous political economic analyses of the commercial influence on U.S. news media, Edward S. Herman and Noam Chomsky's book, *Manufacturing Consent: The Political Economy of Mass Media*, has celebrated its thirtieth anniversary. Herman and Chomsky followed seminal research by Walter Lippmann and Harold Lasswell and posited a propaganda model of media in which content is shaped by five filters, described as ownership, advertising, sourcing, flak, and anti-communism.[8] These five filters represent the overall constraints of market pressures, ownership, and organizational structures, as well as political power on media performance.

The "ownership" filter is set by the expectations of the "large, profit-seeking corporations" that are owned and "controlled by very wealthy people or by managers who are subject to sharp constraints by owners and other market-profit-oriented forces, and they are closely interlocked, and have important common interests with other major corporations, banks and government."[9] Accordingly, there are inherent conflicts of interest built into the media system based on ownership and the demands for increasing wealth, which tends to constrain news content in the interest of profits, as well as concern for other investments.

Closely related to ownership pressures is the advertising filter. As described by Herman and Chomsky, advertising can function as a "de facto licensing authority"[10] that limits content based on the interests of advertisers, but also limits access to content that is produced by advertising-supported news outlets.[11] As Herman and Chomsky explained, news media that lack advertising are put at a "serious disadvantage" in the marketplace because their prices for subscription will be "high, curtailing sales, and they will have less surplus to invest improving the salability" of their product, such as "features, attractive format, promotion, etc."[12] Furthermore, "an advertising-based system will tend to drive out of existence or into marginality the media companies and types that depend on revenue from sales alone."[13] The significance of advertising in the news business has also contributed to the increasing concentration of media ownership, as outlets with greater horizontal and vertical reach have more market range and can compete more aggressively for national advertising, while leaving competitors without such interlocking interests in the margins.

Separate from the demands of ownership and advertising is the "sourcing" filter of the propaganda model described by Herman and Chomsky, which refers to what may often become the symbiotic relationship between news media and powerful sources of information, and their mutual need for one another. News media are reliant on credible sources of information on a regular basis to fill the daily schedules of newspapers and television outlets, and government and corporate sources are "credible for their status and prestige."[14] At the same time, these sources are aware of their power and may leverage it through threats to cut off access to news media or inundate the media with "a particular line and frame" for its stories.[15] Sourcing as a news filter in this sense can be summarized as the media's reliance on particular powerful sources of information, as well as the status conferred upon them as being credible ones.

The "flak" filter is described as political spin, as well as the negative responses to news reporting that powerful interests find unfavorable. As Herman and Chomsky explained, those with influence can "work on the media indirectly by complaining to their own constituencies" and generate advertising that does the same, as well as "funding right-wing monitoring or think-tank operations designed to attack the media."[16] Most notably, perhaps, is that Herman and Chomsky described governmental entities as a major producer of flak by "regularly assailing, threatening and 'correcting' the media."[17]

The fifth and final filter described by Herman and Chomsky is "anti-communism" as an ideology practiced and propagated by those in power, as communism "threatens the very root of their class position and superior status."[18] Herman and Chomsky explained further that this kind of pro-Western capitalism ideology "helps mobilize the populace against an enemy, and because the concept is fuzzy it can be used against anybody advocating policies that threaten property interests."[19] Moreover, because any triumph of communism is perceived as "the worst imaginable result" in conflicts, especially abroad, "the support of fascism" can be viewed as a "lesser evil."[20] Although Herman and Chomsky's work was published before the collapse of the Soviet Union in Russia, in a broader sense the anti-communism filter can be seen as a pro-capitalism ideology that worries about the growth of socialistic ideas.

Fourteen years after their 1988 book, Herman and Chomsky revisited their model and acknowledged that the internet and developing media platforms appeared to be breaking up some of "the corporate stranglehold on journalism and opening an unprecedented era of interactive democratic media."[21] However, Herman and Chomsky also note that despite the internet's value as additional platform for "dissident and protesters" it is limited as a tool for the critical information needs for many in the public, who lack access and knowledge for effective use.[22] Furthermore, the privatization, commercialization, and concentration of control over internet hardware and platforms "threaten to limit any future prospects of the Internet as a democratic media vehicle."[23]

As Herman and Chomsky acknowledged in 2002, internet-based media operate differently than legacy news media, and online communication has not lived up to its early emancipatory expectations. It could thus be logically re-asserted that corporate media continue to play a central role in the production of news and information as the primary providers of mass-distributed content. However, we might question in the two decades following Herman and Chomsky's 2002 revisit of their propaganda model: has user-generated content via social media outlets, such as Twitter and Facebook, changed this dynamic? While Twitter and Facebook are another iteration of corporate form, does the proliferation of user-generated content sharing on their networks disrupt the centrality of their institutional power?

These questions beg further analysis of the online media ecology to understand and perhaps reformulate Herman and Chomsky's original five filters to address the way digital intermediaries, particularly social media, and user-generated content have affected traditional information value chains, such as the process of content production, discovery and distribution, as well as the how that process is monetized by advertising and data vending. Accordingly, the political economic analysis of fake news on social media, applying (and reforming) Herman and Chomsky's original propaganda model, will be a valuable addition to the critical study of how digital technologies have been used to transform journalism.

The 2016 presidential election and the rise of fake news, which occurred another fourteen years after they revisited and republished their model, provides a ripe opportunity to re-apply the model and critically examine how new online media platforms have affected the delivery of news and information. Similar to the original 1988 propaganda model, the analysis to be presented in this chapter will focus on "media structure and performance, not the effects of the media on the public" and this analysis does not imply that fake news, or other elements of the model, are always effective.[24] Moreover, in their republished edition, Herman and Chomsky noted several limitations of internet media—primarily the growth and prominence of brand names and commercial organization.[25] As Herman and Chomsky put it: "People watch and read in good part on the basis of what is readily available and intensively promoted."[26] This assertion begs for further political economic analysis in the current fake news and post-truth environment.

Applying the propaganda model to fake news: a political economic critique

In applying Herman and Chomsky's classic propaganda model to the new terrain of fake news on social media, this chapter employs a political economic critique of social media activity, focusing on the U.S. presidential election contest between Republican Donald Trump and Democrat Hillary Clinton in 2016, as well as its aftermath. Herman and Chomsky explained that their propaganda model was an analytic framework to interpret U.S. media performance based upon the "institutional structures and relationships within which they operate" that showed how media tend to serve "the powerful societal interests that control and finance them."[27] While Herman and Chomsky were looking at the entire U.S. media system, this analysis applies that model to contemporary social media platforms.

While a shared reality exists on social media that can be measured in terms of the number of "likes," "shares," or "followers" that an account has, it is more challenging to understand how technology, business, and other forces under the surface shape these measures. However, political economy's critical realism is ideally suited to expose these kinds of elusive structural processes.[28]

In addressing the structural processes of social media, the analysis presented here follows Thomas Corrigan's suggestion to further utilize trade press and popular reporting in data research.[29] This study applies Herman and Chomsky's 1998 propaganda model to the contemporary social media environment using data from social media companies, an array of legal documents, including Congressional testimony and grand jury indictments, as well as examples drawn from social media content and trade press reporting.

Ownership and advertising: the business of fake news

As noted earlier, "bots" are automated software programs that operate on social media platforms. They perform specific tasks, such as making posts, and give the illusion of representing a real person interacting and engaging on social media. For instance, two of the most popular conservative Twitter pundits during the 2016 U.S. Presidential election cycle, each with tens of thousands of followers, were outed as Russian trolls.[30] As Samuel Woolley and Douglas Guilbeault showed in their social network analysis, bots can be used to "manufacture consensus by giving the illusion of significant online popularity in order to build real political support" for particular candidates or perspectives.[31]

Woolley and Guilbeault do not suggest that there is some form of direct effect at play here. Nonetheless, bot-generated messages do represent, perhaps, a new form of "agenda-setting" function in that the tweets and memes do not necessarily cause social media users to think differently about the issues referenced in the messages, but the repetition of similar themes and messages appearing in social media feeds likely means that we are thinking about those particular issues, and those issues become salient ones.[32] Throughout the campaign season bot-generated posts provided a prevalence of a certain kind of framing about candidates and issues. A Buzzfeed study showed that fake news on Facebook generated more engagement than regular news sources during the last 3 months of the 2016 presidential campaign.[33] Notably, the "20 top-performing false election stories from hoax sites and hyper-partisan blogs generated 8,711,000 shares, reactions, and comments on Facebook."

As discussed in a previous chapter, Bloomberg News reported that an engineering manager at Twitter discovered a hoard of spam accounts, which happened to be from Russia and Ukraine, in 2015, but the company did not delete them because its growth numbers would be diminished if the accounts were deleted. The accounts (fake or not) were counted as part of its total universe of users, and thus helped inflate Twitter's company value. Twitter, with its 300 million users, is competing with Facebook and its 2 billion users; and shaving off spam accounts would hurt their stock prices, as investors are constantly looking for and rewarding growth.[34] In Congressional testimony, the estimated number of fake accounts from Russia number over 36,000. According to data obtained by the *New York Times* from social media companies,

Russian propaganda reached over 126 million Facebook users, published over 130,000 messages on Twitter, and uploaded over 1,000 videos on YouTube.[35]

While it is difficult to directly quantify the impact of those ads, propaganda, and misinformation, Herman and Chomsky limited their analysis to "media structure and performance, not the effects of the media on the public." Furthermore, "the propaganda model describes forces that shape what the media does; it does not imply that any propaganda emanating from the media is always effective."[36]

Still, the manufactured repetition of themes and messages is problematic, especially as social media, like most legacy media, is dominated by a small group of powerful, far-reaching platforms, such as Facebook (which also owns Instagram), YouTube, and Twitter. Herman and Chomsky noted in their updated propaganda model the continuing "centralization and concentration" of media ownership, and a similar observation can be made about a social media oligopoly that concentrates power within a handful of the most popular platforms.[37]

In Herman and Chomsky's analysis of the "advertising filter" in news, they noted that when news is cheaper, or in recent cases "free," it tends to make those news outlets more accessible to the public, and thus more popular.[38] Legacy news media, particularly the old newspaper model that was heavily subsidized by advertising (particularly classified advertising), has been steadily waning since the growth of free news sources online. Furthermore, the classified advertising dollars left newspapers as job listing services, apartment rentals, and other types of listings moved to more specialized services online. In order to stay in business, most newspapers had to increase their subscription costs online. In contrast, fake news propagated through social media sites is free, and easier to access. Perhaps, confusing things further, traditional news media also use social media platforms to share legitimate news content.

To make the matter even more vexing, there are businesses such as 500views.com that sell views, likes, and dislikes.[39] In other words, social media users pay for services to "like" their posts, and thus increase their popularity (albeit artificially). One of these companies, Devumi.com, sold more than 196 million YouTube views over a three-year period from 2014 to 2017, which included the U.S. presidential campaign season.

> Devumi's customers included an employee of RT, a media orga-
> nization funded by the Russian government, and an employee of
> Al Jazeera English, another state-backed company. Other buyers
> were a filmmaker working for Americans for Prosperity, a conser-
> vative political advocacy group, and the head of video at *The New
> York Post*.[40]

The system uses bot-generated traffic, as well as pop-under videos, on the computers of unsuspecting viewers. The owner-operator of 500views. com claimed that by 2014 "his website was on the first page of Google search results for buying YouTube views" and was selling between 150 and 200 orders a day, "bringing in more than $30,000 a month."

While these examples bring some light to the concentration of sources and artificiality of news and information presented through social media, the "sourcing" and "flak" filters described by Herman and Chomsky need to be applied to further understand the impact of these ownership and advertising mechanisms, particularly in the context of the 2016 U.S. presidential election cycle.

Sourcing and flak: understanding fake news and doublespeak

While Herman and Chomsky's analysis viewed "sourcing" as an activity performed by news media in their selection of stories and sources, when examining social media this function works in two ways.[41] As described in the previous section, a sourcing function occurs in the manipulation of reach and popularity through bots and the vending of likes and dislikes. For instance, a study of over 10 million tweets from 70,000 Twitter accounts found that 6.6 million tweets linked to fake news and conspiracy news publishers in the month before the November 2016 election, and that 65 percent of the fake news links went to a group of just 10 sites.[42]

However, a more dynamic form of sourcing occurs through social media in the form of individual users exercising their personal discretion to like and re-tweet and post similar themes and messages on their own. A data study reported in FiveThirtyEight examined why Americans shared millions of tweets from a single well-funded Russian troll factory, known as the Internet Research Agency (IRA), which ran a sophisticated campaign to "sow disinformation and discord into American politics via social media."[43] FiveThirtyEight showed that IRA troll activity peaked on October 6, 2016, right before WikiLeaks released Hillary Clinton's campaign emails.[44] Moreover, Darren Linvill and Patrick Warren's analysis provided more insight into why the deluge of troll activity was so effective, as the IRA managed to mimic an array of entities across the political spectrum, including Black Lives Matter activists, the Democratic Party, Trump supporters expressing virulent anti-immigration sentiments, and local American news outlets.[45] Ironically, for Americans who were attempting to source different political perspectives on social media (either intentionally or not), they were most likely exposed to the work product of a single Russian-based troll factory. To further the illusion, IRA worked across different online platforms to acquire and repurpose abandoned social media accounts (once created by real people) because these kinds of accounts look more real.[46]

While it appears that market forces (including ownership and advertising) and sourcing are still significant elements in the application of Herman and Chomsky's propaganda model, what they described as "flak" may have become the most momentous factor in the contemporary manufacture of not only consent, but perhaps, the constitution of truth itself.[47] Flak can be seen as more than just political spin, but fake news itself, and the form of doublespeak Trump engages in when talking about what is (and is not) fake news, as well as his denigrating attacks on journalists and journalism. President Trump regularly stoked hatred and distrust of news media by frequently describing the press and reporters as "dishonest," "scum," "horrible people," and "sleaze."[48] These slurs clearly resonated with his supporters during campaign rallies, but they became particularly troubling in blurring the lines of truth, as Trump has used the phrase "fake news" as a form of doublespeak to refer to pro-fessional news outlets that produce stories unfavorable to his campaign and administration. Together, fake news and Trumpian doublespeak have created a treacherous post-truth environment for the institution of journalism.

Facebook itself has also engaged in a form of flak that sought to discredit critics of the social media network for being manipulated by foreign agents in Russia during the 2016 presidential election. Facebook hired "Definers," a Washington, D.C.–based firm, to monitor news coverage of the social media network and produce information to counter its critics' claims. "Definers pressed reporters to explore the financial connections" between its critics and "Color of Change, an online racial justice organization . . . although no grants had been made by the group to support the campaign against Facebook."[49] That Facebook responded to criticism over its platform being used a conduit for Russian interfer-ence in the 2016 presidential election, as well as Cambridge Analytica's appropriation of its consumer database, with a flak campaign of its own to "divert attention to critics and competitors" raises questions about its ability to fairly mediate discourse.[50]

Interestingly, in contrast to Twitter and Facebook's manipulation during the 2016 presidential election cycle, and contrary to the findings presented earlier in this book, President Trump has asserted the opposite—that social media is biased against conservative perspectives.[51]

Sophistry, the ideology of post-truth, and epistemic crisis

Herman and Chomsky explain the force of "anti-communism" ideology in their 1988 propaganda model, and pro-capitalism in their 2002 iter-ation. However, in the realm of social media it seems that the sophistic nature of fake news has created another kind of ideological problem by frustrating the notion of truth and the validity of knowledge.

Douglas Kellner described "postmodern sophistry" as a form of dis-course that occurs in a relativist cultural environment, which accepts that all discourse is laden with biases—thus, one proposition is no more or less credible or valid than another.[52] Everything is relative, and thus there can be no right or wrong, fact or falsity, truth or lie. Hence, postmodern sophistry thrives in a post-truth environment.

The problem presented by post-truth is, perhaps, further vexed in a society that values free expression, as provided under the First Amendment to the U.S. Constitution:

> Congress shall make no law respecting an establishment of religion, or prohibiting the free exercise thereof; or abridging the freedom of speech, or of the press; or the right of the people peaceably to assemble, and to petition the Government for a redress of grievances.[53]

Only in extremely rare circumstances, such as blackmail, fraud, child pornography, harassment, or incitement can criminal penalties be imposed on speech. Moreover, political speech in particular is at the heart of what the First Amendment is supposed to protect, and political speech is often opinion, or belief in something that cannot necessarily be proven true or false. Thus, speech that includes false information or lies is most often protected.

Rather, U.S. jurisprudence has become fond of the "marketplace of ideas" metaphor, the self-righting process, and the belief that truth will always win out over false ideas. Justice Brandeis and courts have long said that the way to address falsehood, fallacies, and lies is with more speech, speech that is true. However, the concern presented here is that fake news may have exposed a fatal flaw in the marketplace of ideas metaphor—the truth may not always emerge in a social media environment prone to sophistic manipulation.

Justice Brandeis himself said that education is the key to making the marketplace of ideas metaphor work. People need to be educated, and willing and able to engage in critical discourse. Moreover, Brandeis asserted that the news media is a key to fostering an educated and well-informed public. If it is, then the public needs to be able to tell the difference between what is real and what is fake, what is true and what is false. While there are professional codes of ethics for journalists, such as those provided by the Society of Professional Journalists and Radio Television Digital News Association, there are none for everyday social media users or social media platforms. If only journalists who subscribe to professional codes of ethics are accountable for reporting the truth, it will matter little if audiences are not listening.

Re-examining Herman and Chomsky's famous propaganda model in light of the fake news era prompted an urgent analysis of the impact of fake news on the epistemic reputation of journalism. From this political economic analysis of fake news sites, bot technology, and the Twitter rhetoric of Donald Trump during his presidential election campaign and presidency, it appears that market forces (including ownership and advertising) and self-censorship (e.g., sourcing and anti-communism) are still significant elements in the application of Herman and Chomsky's propaganda model. Whether or not there was malicious political intent at play with the production of fake news stories to sway voters' opinions (e.g., reports about Russians micro-targeting key voting districts in Wisconsin, Michigan, Ohio, and Pennsylvania with fake news stories on Facebook); there was nonetheless a commercial incentive to produce stories (fake or not) with salacious headlines that would cater to information bias, and more importantly, draw "clicks" and consequently, advertising dollars for the producers of such content. The clicks may help measure cash, but not quality or truth.

Fake news, bots, and doublespeak about what is and isn't "fake news" may have exposed a fatal flaw in the metaphor, as the truth doesn't necessarily emerge in a bot-generated barrage of sophistic tweets, posts, and memes. Furthermore, Brandeis asserted that the news media is key to fostering an educated and well-informed public to make the marketplace of ideas work. In the post-truth world, though, journalism's epistemic status is diminished, as a news audience with appropriate critical literacy skills is needed *before* journalism can perform its epistemic function.

Sue Robinson has suggested that journalists expand their productive space beyond newsrooms by "building presence in all of the citizen-dominated spaces of the Web; instead of using Twitter or Facebook to merely link back to homepages, move into these spaces as new homes to create fully operational news realms outside of the traditional singular home page."[54] This approach is also problematic, as it too easily invites the notion that "we're all journalists now," and therefore, every so-called journalist is as equally credible as any other. Thinking that because we all have access to social media we are all journalists is likely to beget more confusion about what is and is not journalism.

Just because one has the tools to tell stories, does not necessarily mean that one can effectively practice journalism. We posit here that we need to reclaim journalism as an epistemic community. Good investigative journalism will allow us to derive the meaning of what we are reading from what otherwise might seem to be isolated bits of information.

We also need a news audience that appreciates and supports journalism, and values accurate and credible information. Audiences need to know their sources of information, and take responsibility for what they communicate to others, whether it is a share, a like, or a re-tweet. Bots, algorithms, corporate powers, and political interests manufacture versions of reality as truth, and we too often swim through these uncritically. For instance, Sam Wineburg and colleagues found in a study of middle-school-aged children through college students that they were typically unable to understand the differences in credibility among online information sources or tell the difference between advertisements and news stories.[55] Alison Head and colleagues found that nearly half of college students did not feel comfortable telling the differences between real and fake news on social media; and even more concerning, 36 percent distrusted all media because of the possibility of misinformation.[56]

As Herman and Chomsky noted, one of the strengths of the U.S. media system is that there is space for dissent from popular governmental narratives, although it is relegated to the "back pages of the newspapers," so to speak, and discoverable to only the most "diligent and skeptical researcher."[57] Still, there is capacity within the system for the volume of facts to expand. The problem of course is that will matter very little unless facts are given proper attention in terms of "placement, tone and repetition," as well as appropriate context within the media system.

And, moreover, there has to be a critically minded and journalistically literate news audience to interpret and digest the meaning of those facts.

Too often society seems to look for technological solutions to the problems technology creates. For instance, it has been suggested that algorithms may be created to detect fake news. However, as professors Gary Marcus and Ernest Davis explained in a recent *New York Times* op-ed, the idea that artificial intelligence platforms would be able to detect fake news "would require a number of major advances in A.I., taking us far beyond what has so far been invented."[58] Moreover, algorithms that would be employed to detect fake news are imperfect when it comes to the detection of context and nuance, resulting in "panoptic missorts" with troubling results.[59]

Social media, social problems, and social justice

Given the political economic limitations of the digital marketplace of ideas described in this chapter, particularly related to national politics, questions must be raised about how social media is prone to manipulation around social problems and social justice efforts. Just as fake news played a critical role in the 2016 presidential election, similar concerns are present in the realm of social justice, as the largest Black Lives Matter page on Facebook was found to be a fake one.[60]

In January 2019 a fake account on Twitter flamed controversy around a Catholic high school in Covington, Kentucky with a viral video showing students wearing "Make America Great Again" hats while confronting a Native American man in Washington, D.C.[61] The initial tweet went out from an account that appeared to belong to a San Francisco-area schoolteacher named "Talia" with the handle @2020fight.[62] The tweet stated, "This MAGA loser gleefully bothering a Native American protestor at the Indigenous Peoples March," and included a tightly edited video of the confrontation. That infamous tweet received at least 2.5 million views, over 27,000 likes and over 14,000 retweets, according to a *USA Today* analysis of over 3 million tweets and thousands of Facebook posts that went out in the moments after the original video.[63] While the account purportedly belonged to a California teacher, Twitter later determined that it actually originated from Brazil and had an inordinate number of followers (approximately 40,000) for a non-celebrity, similar to the fake "Jenna Abrams" account described earlier.

Another suspected fake account (this one on Facebook) also helped to fan the flames of the same Covington Catholic controversy. In the early morning hours of January 19, a Facebook page called "Real Mexican Problems" posted the same video and attracted over a million views, as well as over 20,000 shares.[64] This Facebook page was created in 2013 with a self-described mission to "abolish white supremacy." However, the contact information for the page lists a phone number for the White Knights of the Ku Klux Klan—an obvious red flag for its authenticity.

Later, another (and much longer) video emerged from a group of Black Hebrew Israelites, who were present during the incident on the National Mall in Washington, and provides more details, context, and nuance than the original video that went viral. Furthermore, the longer video that emerged after national outrage focused on the Covington Catholic High School students contradicted claims made in the original viral post, as the Black Hebrew Israelites were taunting Native Americans and the Covington students before the Native American man (later identified as Nathan Phillips) is clearly seen marching into the crowd of Covington students.

Another way to look at the incident that took place on January 18, 2019 is that there were three different groups of people (high school students from a conservative Catholic high school in Kentucky, Native Americans, and Black Hebrew Israelites) from widely different cultures, with contrasting world views, exercising their First Amendment rights on the National Mall in ways (that in at least in two cases) were patently offensive. Absent social media and the original viral video, this would not be a news story.

However, with social media, a fake social media account was able to ignite national outrage over the incident by presenting it within a narrow frame of cultural politics. When the later video emerged that showed the students were not the only aggressors in the incident, this did little to quash widespread anger at the students, as individual perceptions of the "truth" of the event had already been manufactured through their social media feeds.

Accordingly, the next chapter examines the manipulation of social justice activities on social media, and its engagement with national cultural politics throughout the summer of 2020 leading up to the U.S. Capitol riot on January 6, 2021.

chapter 9

social justice,
national cultural politics,
and the summer of 2020

Editor's note: As with Chapter 6, the QR code below will take you to the freely available online edition of the chapter. By following the link provided by this QR code, you will be able to engage with the cited figures that do not appear in this print version. Because the findings are expertly summarized in this edition, you will not be at risk of missing any of the analysis by not looking at the cited figures. Figure references are consistent between both the print and online editions.

https://bit.ly/33vVqVa

Throughout our study of social media and social justice movements, we have endeavored to enhance our methodologies through the course of each data set. As we progressed through each of these cases (Ferguson in 2014, the 2016 election, and now 2020), the network dynamics are more complex, and thus more advanced methods are required. At first, in the Ferguson case, we looked at acute, punctuated moments around a particular event in which social justice efforts intersected with the engagement of social media and showed the potential for how social justice groups may use social media to reshape communicative power.

We then moved on to broader movements in politics and examined network behavior over time, how things go viral, how networks can be affected, and what social justice groups can learn from how the political right engages in network activity. From this data we were able to demonstrate how pro-Trump actors were more effective in attracting attention and dominating activity on Twitter through centralizing their themes and employing similar hashtags.

Reflecting on these previous cases, Ferguson in 2014, which demonstrated the political potential of social media for social justice groups; and the 2016 election campaign, which showed how a right-leaning political faction can dominate a social media network despite being outnumbered—we now ask whether social justice groups (and the political left) are too fractured as social networks to be an effective political force. Furthermore, we considered how the political right was engaged in left-leaning social justice movements taking shape on Twitter. We look to some of the events that shaped the early summer of 2020 to find these answers, after three separate killings of Black people occurred within months of each other in different cities across the U.S. Protests peaked after the death of George Floyd on May 25 in Minneapolis, as the fallout from earlier shootings of Ahmaud Arbery in Georgia (in February) and Breonna Taylor in Louisville (in March) began to take shape. Events surrounding all three killings converge in late May and early June of 2020.

Ahmaud Arbery

On February 23, 2020, an unarmed Black man, Ahmaud Arbery, who was out jogging in Brunswick, Georgia, was confronted by a white father and son before being fatally shot as another white companion video-recorded the carnage on his phone. The video of Arbery's murder was released on May 5, 2020, and quickly went viral, sparking outcry over racial profiling by the white men, including one who was a former police officer in the Georgia county in which Ahmaud's killing occurred.

On May 7, 2020, the father and son (Gregory and Travis McMichael) were arrested for Ahmaud's murder; two weeks later, their neighbor who recorded the shooting, William Bryan, was arrested (on May 21, 2020). The latest arrest occurred at the same time that another killing of an unarmed Black person, this time at the hands of police, was gaining national awareness, as protests kept sustained attention on these events.[1]

Breonna Taylor

In the early morning hours of March 13, 2020, Breonna Taylor, a 26-year-old Black woman, was shot and killed in her Louisville, Kentucky apartment by plainclothes police officers, who were serving a no-knock search warrant (at the wrong residence). The actual targets of the search warrant were in another dwelling several miles away. On May 15, Taylor's family filed a wrongful death lawsuit against the officers involved in the shooting and the city of Louisville, as protests over Taylor's death continued in the city for months. During a June 1 demonstration in Louisville, a Black business owner, David McAtee, was shot and killed by police who had failed to wear or activate their body cameras, prompting the firing of the city's chief of police and further heightening attention on social justice movements taking place in cities across the U.S.[2]

George Floyd

The ongoing outcry over the deaths of Ahmaud Arbery and Breonna Taylor congealed in the aftermath of George Floyd's killing by Minneapolis police officer Derek Chauvin on May 25, 2020. Videos of Floyd's death captured by onlookers were shared on social media and television news outlets. The images and audio were potent—showing Floyd pleading that he could not breathe, as bystanders pleaded with Chauvin and other officers standing nearby to show mercy. Floyd was held face down on the street with his hands cuffed behind his back as Chauvin pressed his knee into Floyd's neck. Floyd ultimately became unresponsive and died. The brutality of Floyd's detention was disproportionate to the reason for his arrest—concern that he had tried to pass a counterfeit $20 dollar bill at a convenience store. Disquiet over the untimely deaths of Arbery, Taylor, and Floyd, as well as other unarmed Black people, culminated in thousands of people taking to the streets across big cities and small towns across America in late May and throughout June under the banner "Black Lives Matter."

This moment was also met by counter-protesters from the political right, including a community in Bethel, Ohio that made international headlines.[3] Over these weeks the markers of social justice, such as #BlackLivesMatter, #EnoughIsEnough, and #ICantBreathe clashed on Twitter with counter-emblems of the political right, including #BackTheBlue, #BlueLivesMatter, #AllLivesMatter, as well as Trump specific campaign hashtags, #MAGA, #KAG, and #Trump. As such, it was an opportune period of time to further explore how power operates in contestations over social justice and cultural politics on social media. While social media demonstrated great potential as a platform for social justice advocates to reframe public discourse during Ferguson in 2014, the political right also showed the strength of its social networking in the 2016 election season. Now in the summer of 2020, both forces from left-leaning social justice movements and the Trump-led political right (fueled by another presidential election campaign) collided on Twitter. How did social justice advocates fare on social media when engaged by a strongly congealed network of the political right?

Procedures for analysis

As before, we completed a set of data visualizations to examine this question. This third set of data visualizations covers two important periods in May of 2020: after the video of Arbery's murder was released on May 5, and after Floyd's killing on May 25, when activity on Twitter was peppered with tweets and hashtags about the deaths of Arbery, Taylor, and Floyd, as well as the 2020 presidential campaign. Building upon our core methodology developed in chapters 3 and 6 in this book, this set of Twitter data visualizations is derived from the Twitter historical archive. We explored tweet-retweet relationships, and provided basic descriptive statistics about Twitter activity. The tweet-retweet relationships are featured as an array of nodes, which consists of users in the searched data, and links are built between those users and others who retweeted them.

Originally, we sought to create a set of network visualizations for time periods following the killings, including the five days following Taylor's shooting (March 13–17), five days following the video footage released of Arbery's killing (May 5–9), and five days following Floyd's death (May 26–30). However, there was not a comparable amount of Twitter activity during the March dates, while the other two data sets from May yielded overwhelming results due to their size. The latter of the two sets of data for May (following Floyd's killing) were too large to render for a five-day period, so we only sampled two days (May 26–27) for this network so that it can be used more easily in the interactive data sets presented below. The data visualization dashboards provided online allow for interactive explorations of the data collected (see the URLs below for data sets 1a–1e and 2a–2b). Building off our procedures in Chapter 6, we also present the centrality of the major nodes in both degree and betweenness, as represented through numerical data and visual representations of these networks. You can also see the frequency with which a specified Twitter handle uses a particular hashtag and the rate at which that hashtag co-occurs within the handles' network.

Data sets 1a–1e: Ahmaud Arbery

Data set # 1a: May 5, 2020
   https://themlmom.com/projects/debates?ahmaudarbery_5
Data set # 1b: May 6, 2020
   https://themlmom.com/projects/debates?ahmaudarbery_6
Data set # 1c: May 7, 2020
   https://themlmom.com/projects/debates?ahmaudarbery_7
Data set # 1d: May 8, 2020
   https://themlmom.com/projects/debates?ahmaudarbery_8
Data set # 1e: May 9, 2020
   https://themlmom.com/projects/debates?ahmaudarbery_9

Data sets # 2a–2b: George Floyd

Data set # 2a: May 26, 2020
      https://themlmom.com/projects/debates?georgefloyd_26
Data set # 2b: May 27, 2020
      https://themlmom.com/projects/debates?georgefloyd_27

Scan this QR code for the online version of Chapter 9, where you can view the live links for these datasets

In analyzing the hashtags employed by Twitter users throughout data sets 1a–1e and 2a and 2b we adapted the schemas presented and discussed in Chapter 3.[4] From the data presented in this chapter, we considered the varying hashtags to be in one of three categories: victim names, social justice ideological/conceptual markers, and political right ideological/conceptual markers (see Figure 9.1 below). "Victim names" were hashtags that were either #BreonnaTaylor, #AhmaudArbery, or #GeorgeFloyd. These were simply markers that made a factual reference to the victim. In the "social justice" category were hashtags that implied an ideological belief in support of social justice (e.g., #BlackLivesMatter) or made a personal conceptualization of the killing (e.g., #ICantBreathe). "Political right" hashtags were ones that suggested political beliefs counter to the social justice movement (e.g., #BackTheBlue) and were often used in tandem with pro-Trump campaign tags (e.g., #MakeAmericaGreatAgain and #KeepAmericaGreat).

It should be noted in our schemas described above and presented in Figure 9.1 below that these are not necessarily mutually exclusive categories. For instance, in Blevins et al. (2019) and again in Chapter 3, the ideological and conceptual markers were separate groupings.[5] In the case of Ferguson, we separated ideological markers, such as #BlackLivesMatter, from conceptual ones, such as #IfTheyGunnedMeDown, to isolate the phenomenon of individuals who noted how their race or color would be implicated in an officer-involved shooting. These conceptual markers were often used in conjunction with ideological ones supporting social justice, which is why we collapsed the two categories into one when looking at the data in this chapter. We noted a similar pairing in these data sets with political right markers and pro-Trump tags. Moreover, we were also cognizant of the hashtag hijacking strategies described in Chapter 5 that have been applied by both social justice advocates and political-right pro-Trump forces.

Victim names	Social justice	Political right
#BreonnaTaylor	#BLM	#AllLivesMatter
#AhmaudArbery	#BlackLivesMatter	#BlueLivesMatter
#GeorgeFloyd	#policebrutality	#BackTheBlue
	#EnoughIsEnough	#MAGA
	#ICantBreath	#MakeAmericaGreatAgain
	#SayHerName	#KAG
	#SayHisName	#KeepAmericaGreat
	#JusticeForBreonna Taylor	#Trump
	#JusticeForAhmaudArbery	
	#JusticeForGeorgeFloyd	

Figure 9.1
Hashtag Schemas

Prominence of victim names in the hashtags

The hashtag #AhmaudArbery dwarfs all others on May 5, 2020. It is in the center of the network and prominent throughout its perimeter as well (see Figure 9.2 online via the QR code at the beginning of the chapter). Moreover, it remains the dominant hashtag in the days that follow.

By May 9, 2020, though, three other hashtags grow more prominent in the network, including #SeanReed, #SayHerName, #JusticeForBreonnaTaylor, and #BlackLivesMatter (see Figure 9.3).

Figure 9.3 (across spread)

Most used hashtags on May 9, 2020

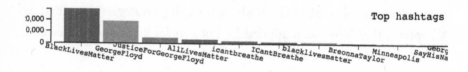

Figure 9.5 (across spread)

Victim names in the network on May 27, 2020

Although the #SayHerName hashtag was initiated during the Sandra Bland case from 2015, it most likely associated with the more recent Breonna Taylor incident during this week of 2020. Bland was found dead in a Texas jail cell after her arrest during a traffic stop. As Owens noted, "the names of too many Black men and boys killed by police—Michael Brown, Eric Garner, Philando Castile, Freddie Gray, Tamir Rice—are widely known, Black women's cases have rarely garnered national attention."[6] Breonna Taylor's killing was one of the exceptions, especially after Ahmaud Arbery's death.

Interestingly, Twitter activity in the aftermath of the release of video showing Arbery's murder also drew attention to lesser-known cases on the national level. Namely, the #SeanReed hashtag referred to Sean Reed's shooting death in Indianapolis on May 6, 2020. Police spotted Reed, a Black U.S. Army veteran, driving erratically and pursued him. Reed started a Facebook Live video during his pursuit by the officers. After fleeing his vehicle, Reed (who was unarmed) was shot several times, and as he lay dead his Facebook Live stream recorded officers joking that his funeral was going to have to be one with a "closed casket".[7]

used in Network

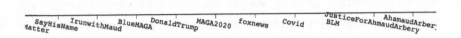

SayHisName   IrunwithMaud   BlueMAGA   DonaldTrump   MAGA2020   foxnews   Covid   Justice   AhamaudArber
Matter   BLM   iceForAhmaudArbery

used in Network

geFloyd   BlackLivesMatters   JusticeForFloyd   PoliceBrutality   RIPGeorgeFloyd   ahmaudarbery   fortheculture   Wipeitdownchallenge   wipeitdown   georgesfloyo
ame   loydWasMurdered

The pattern of tagging the victim's name in posts is also notable in the day after George Floyd's killing (see Figure 9.4 online via the QR code at the beginning of the chapter).

By the second day after Floyd's death, two other names of recent victims become visible in the network's hashtags, including #BreonnaTaylor and #ahmaudarbery (see Figure 9.5). This phenomenon is indicative of a shift in power from media and police defining victims, to affective publics identifying the victims and linking their deaths to the themes of social justice.

Social justice themes throughout the network

What is, perhaps, more significant is that while the #GeorgeFloyd hashtag dominates the network on May 26, it is surpassed by the #BlackLivesMatter tag during the next day on May 27 (see Figure 9.5). Moreover, a broader array of other social-justice-themed hashtags are present in the network, including #JusticeForGeorgeFloyd, #ICantBreathe, #SayHisName, and #PoliceBrutality (see Figure 9.6 online via the QR code at the beginning of the chapter).

One of the more notable tweets on May 27, 2020, that evoked the #ICantBreathe hashtag was produced by @ColorofChange (see Figure 9.7). The tweet combines hashtags that personally identify the victim, #GeorgeFloyd, along with a relevant theme of social justice, #ICantBreathe, as Floyd exclaimed "I can't breathe" while being pinned to the ground. Moreover, #ICantBreathe was not only relevant to the Floyd case; it was first evoked after the death of Eric Garner, another unarmed Black man, who was killed by police officers in New York on July 17, 2014. Garner was approached by police officers for selling single cigarettes and died after an officer restrained him with a chokehold. Like Floyd, Garner had pleaded "I can't breathe" before his death; and also, like Floyd, the violent manner in which he was apprehended by police seemed greatly disproportionate to the crime he was suspected of committing.

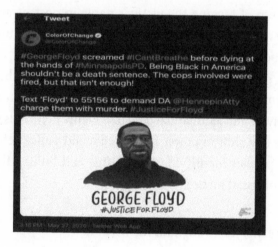

Figure 9.7
@ColorofChange tweet from May 27, 2020

Besides the #BlackLivesMatter hashtag that clearly resonated the most as a theme of social justice after the Floyd killing, another social-justice-themed hashtag of note is #SayHerName. As mentioned earlier, this tag was first used following the death of Sandra Bland in 2015 and it emerged, notably, again in May of 2020 after the Breonna Taylor killing.

The use of the hashtag is remarkable in that it represents the intersection of several social justice themes, while focusing on the underreported victimization of Black women by police violence.[8] However, while the #SayHerName hashtag is employed frequently, it does not occupy a central place in the network, as it is scattered in small pockets and only congeals on the margins (see Figure 9.8 online via the QR code at the beginning of the chapter), which suggests that it did not resonate across the broader network and achieve the kind of popularity that #BlackLivesMatter attained.).

The political right on the margins

Curiously, perhaps, the most prominent political-right hashtag after the viral video release of Ahmaud Arbery's murder was #BlueLivesMatter (see Figure 9.9 online via the QR code at the beginning of the chapter). The #BlueLivesMatter tag has been invoked as a political-right sentiment in response to officer-involved shootings. What seems unusual in this case is that Arbery was not killed by police officers, although one of the assailants was a former police officer. Similarly, the #AllLivesMatter hashtag (see Figure 9.10 online via the QR code at the beginning of the chapter) is another political-right counter sentiment to the #BlackLivesMatter hashtag, which centers blackness in discourses about the killing of unarmed Black people.

Major findings

From the data presented here, we can see that the events of early 2020 resonated broadly on Twitter, as a vast array of Twitter activity linked specific victims to the broader themes of social justice. What is not evident is whether certain social justice groups or accounts associated with the political left were particularly dominant within the network. Rather, the momentum of awareness that built around the cases of Ahmaud Arbery, Breonna Taylor, and George Floyd, as well as their deaths' implicit attachment to the cause of social justice, was so great that otherwise politically fractured networks congealed around a few core messages, including the hashtag #BlackLivesMatter.

There is also evidence here that the political right was actively engaged in counterposing the themes of social justice on Twitter. While those on the political right may have been vastly outnumbered in this case, the data also suggests that they still possess greater solidarity—as a political force—than those on the left. We then must ask, what does this mean for the potential use of social media for social justice in the future? How may the political economy of online networks shape this future? We address these questions in our concluding chapter.

chapter 10

conclusions

The political economy of social media and social justice

Our findings presented in Chapter 3 from Ferguson in 2014 provided some optimism about the power and potential of social media for advocates of social justice. However, data presented in chapters 6 and 9 demonstrated more generally how power operates on social media, as other political forces can be just as influential, if not more so. While social justice themes were prominently displayed on Twitter in the summer of 2020, the political right was active in countering those messages. Notably, while the handles and hashtags associated with the political right were smaller in number on Twitter during critical moments of 2020, they also appeared to have greater political solidarity than those associated with social justice, and on the political left. The themes of social justice were greater in number and more diverse, but we are left to wonder what the future holds for social media and social justice. Moreover, how may the broader political and economic environment of online networks shape the potential effectiveness of social media for social justice? Based on the data presented through each of the cases explored in this book, as well as our wider political-economic analyses, concerns remain about the solidity of political right networks, as well as misinformation spread and the manipulation of information about social justice on social media.

Congealed political right networks

As Jessica Mahone and Philip Napoli showed, the political right has built a network of hyper-partisan news websites (and many with accompanying social media assets) that appear as independent local news outlets.[1] While there were a small number of left-leaning partisan news sites, they were dwarfed by their right-leaning counterparts by more than 400 to 8. Mahone and Napoli based their study on previous work by Priyanjana Bengani, who showed that just a handful of corporate entities operate a network of 450 news sites across 12 states.[2] This is another illustration of how right-leaning political interests are more congealed in their efforts, and able to produce a digital echo-chamber of similar themes and messages. Alexander Stewart and colleagues fielded a role-playing game experiment that underscored the significance of this phenomenon in which a "small number of zealots, when strategically placed on the influence network" can engage in what the authors call "information gerrymandering."[3]

Moreover, it appears that power may be appreciably affected by unity. As shown in our second data sets from Chapter 6, and to a lesser extent in Chapter 9, left-leaning groups do not coalesce around a core set of ideas the way that the political right does. The political right's coalescence tends to increase their effectiveness, even when it is outnumbered by the political left, especially in matters of national cultural politics. Without the same strength of unity as on the political right, social justice advocates and the political left will have to vastly outnumber their opponents in order to prevail with their messaging. While this was possible, as demonstrated in Chapter 9 with the broader racial justice movement in the wake of the George Floyd killing, creating awareness of more marginal social justice issues, such as food insecurity and income inequality, may not be as successful in the future.

Furthermore, the comparative lack of political unity between the left and right likely makes the larger causes of social justice, such as voting rights and racial justice, more prone to manipulation by outside forces.

Information manipulation and misinformation on social media

As reported by CNN, a more insidious form of Russian-backed manipulation took shape on social media early in 2020, similar to that which occurred during the 2016 election campaign. This time the fake social media accounts were even "better disguised and more targeted, harder to identify and track," and based outside of Russia itself—in West African nations.[4] The troll accounts claimed to be in the U.S. and featured handles such as @africamustwake. The accounts would post inflammatory content "focused almost exclusively on racial issues in the US, promoting Black empowerment and often displaying anger towards white Americans," while employing hashtags associated with the social justice movement, such as #BLM, #Racism and #PoliceBrutality. The posts regularly tried to engage actual social justice groups on their own social media platforms, including a Black Lives Matter group in Cincinnati.[5] While Twitter reported that it had taken down more than 70 of these accounts before March of 2020, it is unknown if they later regenerated in another form, or what their impact was on public sentiments leading up to the summer of 2020.

Another potent form of manipulation and misinformation taking place on social media involved a white nationalist group that created a Twitter account posing as a national "antifa" organization.[6] The group, Identity Evropa, made several incendiary, false, or otherwise misleading claims on the account that played into then-president Trump's narrative that so-called "antifa" groups and "radical left" extremist groups were looting and destroying property during demonstrations over George Floyd's death.[7]

The congealed nature of political right networks likely made them more prone to manipulation and misinformation campaigns, especially from one of Twitter's most prominent influencers since 2016, Donald Trump. Reporters, Aamer Madhani and Jill Colvin detailed several of Trump's provocative tweets in the history of his @realDonaldTrump Twitter account.[8] Perhaps none were more consequential than the ones he sent between the November 2020 presidential election and the

Capitol riot in January 2021. In testimony before the U.S. Senate, FBI Director Christopher Wray said that "racially motivated extremists" were behind the Capitol riot and alluded to the role that social media played in their ability to mobilize.[9] It appears that white nationalist and far-right groups, as well as other Trump supporters, coalesced around Trump's misleading messages about election fraud, following a summer of protests about racism and policing.

In the week following Twitter's banishment of Trump and several of his allies from the social media network, Zignal Labs reported that unbased claims of election fraud dropped from 2.5 million to 688,000.[10] Twitter also suspended more than 70,000 of its user accounts that shared content from QAnon, which was a prominent source of baseless conspiracy theories about the 2020 election, as well as other political issues.[11] While the take-down of Trump and purveyors of QAnon conspiracies may have dramatically dropped the spread of misinformation about the election on Twitter, it only did so after the damage was already done via the Capitol riot. Furthermore, this kind of after-the-fact strategy does not address the potential for other forms of information manipulation related to politics or social justice in the future.

However, when trying to proactively manage hate speech on their networks, social media companies have often employed content moderation systems that may not appropriately detect context when interpreting messages. For instance, several Black Facebook users complained that their posts about racism were censored as hate speech by the network's content moderation system.[12] These systems may lack the nuance to know the difference between posts about experiencing or decrying racism and those that are actively promoting it. These kinds of misinterpretations can occur when algorithmic programs try to dichotomize information and wrongly "fix its cultural meaning."[13] This still leaves us with the thorny problem of how to effectively deal with the manipulation of information on social media networks in a way that provides depth and clarity.

A Pew Research Center study showed that Americans viewed fake news and misinformation as a major problem (rating it ahead of illegal immigration and terrorism), blamed politicians for the crisis, but expect journalists to fix it.[14] Towards that end, several journalists, news, institutions and media scholars have addressed the problem. For instance, Claire Wardle's First Draft organization provides several tools and resources for detecting misinformation online.[15] Another great example is *The Guardian*'s interactive online resource about how specific bits of misinformation spread on social media during riots that occurred in London.[16] While this kind of research from scholars and journalists is useful and insightful, they are nonetheless postmortem exercises after social media misinformation and manipulations have already wreaked their havoc on the narrative of popular politics and the cause of social justice.

The narrative politics of social justice on social media

Shiller described how viral stories, both true and false, can affect broader economic behavior in a process described as "narrative economics."[17] Our study presented here suggests a similar phenomenon involved with the narrative politics of social justice on social media. User posts, likes, and shares of information and misinformation correspond with their political beliefs and choices.

Since the 2000s we have seen the narrative politics of social media swing from the left to the right. During his successful presidential campaigns in 2008 and 2012, Barrack Obama social media monikers of #Hope, #Change and #YesWeCan were unifying themes for the political left.[18] However, successful social media strategies were employed by Donald Trump, who dominated Twitter, and the political right during the 2016 campaign. The political left's influencers were too late to the scene in 2016 and did not possess a theme that galvanized their base the way that #MakeAmericaGreatAgain did for the right.

The narrative politics of social media on social justice movements and white nationalists has also swung from left to right since 2016. The #BlackLivesMatter social justice movement was initially, and successfully, activated using social media through Ferguson in 2014. However, the blend of bots, bad actors, Trump and Trumpism, as well as extreme movements on the political right have since complicated the narrative and meaning of this movement, as demonstrated by what culminated in the U.S. Capitol riot on January 6, 2021. Will the pendulum of narrative politics on social media swing back from right to left, as Twitter's purge of Donald Trump and other QAnon purveyors might suggest?

We argue here that it depends (in part) upon the impact of highly networked individuals in future social justice endeavors, such as Antonio French, a St. Louis alderman who became a trusted source of on-the-ground information during the Ferguson unrest.[19] Our early analysis of Ferguson showed how specific framings may have affected popular perceptions of the events taking place there, as well as a deeper understanding of their cultural meaning. Networks of non-official state actors or affective publics can form and strengthen social justice movements through the production of their own images and interpretive frames.

Social justice activity taking place on social media has been dynamic, as tweets and hashtags not only reflected what was happening on the ground during protests but also helped to construct broader political narratives about the events that led to the protests. In several instances, specific social justice narratives moved from social media into the broader popular culture. For example, the song "Don't Shoot" by American rap artist The Game took its title from the hashtag #HandsUpDontShoot that trended during Ferguson and its lyrics invoke the history of Trayvon Martin, Emmett Till, and others in the wake of the Michael Brown shooting.

Journalists and journalism can continue to shape the narrative politics of social justice on social media too. In Ferguson and throughout the summer of 2020 we saw journalists as eyewitnesses who frequently validated and verified the imagery and experiences that were being shared organically by protestors on social media. Journalists such as Wesley Lowrey and Ryan Reilly, who were arrested while covering Ferguson in 2014,[20] as well as Andrea Sahouri who was arrested in Iowa while covering a Black Lives Matter protest in 2020,[21] became part of the story during these events. The facts of their arrests not only made national headlines, but more importantly, they further chronicled the unjust experiences and encounters that people of color often have with police. Journalists became part of the network of understanding about social justice.

While such common experiences of injustice may tend to make journalists and social justice advocates unexpected allies of sorts in search of the truth, they may also inflame other political narratives, especially by those on the political right. Journalists are supposed to be independent, and not necessarily allies of any other group. As the front line of narrative politics on social media continues to evolve, journalists, social advocates, and the political left would be well served to unify around the themes of social justice, although journalists will need care to maintain their professional autonomy. While social media and other digital communication platforms have empowered social justice movements in important ways, these tools have also been subject to broader political and economic forces, as well as exploitation by hate groups, white nationalists, and other right-wing extremists that are counterposed to social justice.

The open access edition of *Social Media, Social Justice, and the Political Economy of Online Networks* can be found via this QR code

https://bit.ly/3u2Kibr

Please visit https://ucincinnatipress.manifoldapp.org/, to read and engage with our other open access titles and resources.

acknowledgements

This book was a team effort, and I had a great team. It started with recruitment by and continued support of Liz Scarpelli who first reached out to James and me shortly after she became the inaugural director of University of Cincinnati Press in February 2017. She has been in engaged with serving UC and its "Next Lives Here" philosophy the moment she walked in the door. Foremost on Liz's agenda was to foster a twenty-first century academic publishing environment that puts UC scholarship at the cutting edge of innovation. It was her idea to develop an open-access monograph around the work James and I were doing about social justice and political activities taking place on Twitter, and our work benefited from the unique and innovative environment she created for open access publishing. Moreover, Liz is an engaging and critical thinker, and she makes the scholarship taking place under her stewardship better.

One of the best measurements of a leader is the quality of the team that person assembles. In this, case Liz has excelled again with her right-hand woman and managing editor of UC Press, Sarah Muncy, associate editor for this book, Daniel Mattox, and the copy editor, Ann Klefstad. All writers benefit from good editing, and I have enjoyed the thoughtful and diligent oversight of several outstanding editors. And I deeply appreciate the publicity and promotion for this work from Betsy DeJesu and Brandon Waggoner.

I am most grateful for the work of my colleague (and neighbor) Dr. James Lee, who approached me after I had presented a textual analysis of #Ferguson tweets at a University of Cincinnati Digital Media Collaborative retreat in August 2016. He presented a vision for how we could further explore humanistic questions through data-based analysis. James has been a steadfast supporter and entrepreneur for this project and hired two outstanding fellows—Erin E. McCabe (MLIS, Pratt Institute) and Ezra Edgerton (B.A., Grinnell College, Iowa) to support our data collection. Ezra has been an integral part of this project and his methodological work on the data visualizations presented here has contributed immeasurably to this book. Quite simply, I could not have done this without his expertise, and I am thankful to have worked with Ezra on several other projects in which he was a fellow co-author.

In addition to the generous assistance from the Digital Scholarship Center at the University of Cincinnati, our research presented here was supported by gifts from the Andrew W. Mellon Foundation; The Cincinnati Project at the University of Cincinnati, which provided for research assistance from Katie Coburn (while she was an undergraduate student in journalism at UC); and the University of Cincinnati Office of the Provost, which supported this work as an open-access monograph. While the open-access version of this book in 2021 was designed for peer data researchers and other experts, the 2022 print version that you are reading here was written with a more general audience that is intellectually engaged. While the open-access site (available at https://ucincinnatipress.manifoldapp.org/projects/political-discourse-on-social-media) provides more detailed discussion of methodological practice suited for peers who wish to conduct their own analyses from our data sets, the print version includes more narrative about what all of this research means for how we as a society understand the role of social media in social justice movements, popular politics, the economy, and our personal lives.

And speaking of personal lives, throughout this project, and my career, I am especially blessed by the love and partnership of my wife Melissa and our sons Jeff G. and John ("Jack"). Finally, to the many family members, friends, and colleagues who have celebrated each of my professional milestones throughout the years – thank you.

—Jeffrey Layne Blevins (January 21, 2022)

Notes

Chapter 1

1. J. Crump, "The Case Against Trump: A Look at His Tweets from January 6th." *The Independent*, February 12, 2021. https://www.independent.co.uk/news/world/americas/us-politics/trump-tweets-jan-6-impeachment-evidence-b1801715.html

2. K.A. Zimmerman and J. Empsak. "Internet History Timeline: ARPANET to the World Wide Web." *Live Science*, June 27, 2017. https://www.livescience.com/20727-internet-history.html.

3. P. C. O'Brien. "Social Media History and Use." In *Social Media*, edited by K. Langmia et al., xv (New York, NY: University Press of America, 2014).

4. Ibid.

5. Ibid.

6. D. M. Boyd and N. B. Ellison. "Social Network Sites: Definition, History, and Scholarship." *Journal of Computer-Mediated Communication* 13:1 (2007): 210–30.

7. C. Berlet. "When Hate Went Online." Paper presented to the Northeast Sociological Association, Spring Conference at Sacred Heart University in Fairfield, CT, April 28, 2001. http://citeseerx.ist.psu.edu/viewdoc/download?doi=10.1.1.552.239&rep=rep1&type=pdf

8. P. B. Gersten, D. R. Grant, and C. Chiang. "Hate Online: A Content Analysis of Extremist Internet Sites." *Analyses of Social Issues and Public Policy* 3:1 (2003): 30.

9. J. Bonazzo. "Facebook Removes White Nationalist Group Pages After Charlottesville Attack: Twitter and Reddit Face Scrutiny for Allowing Hate Speech." *The Observer*, August 16, 2017. https://observer.com/2017/08/charlottesville-facebook-removes-racist-pages/

10. "Methodology: How hate groups are identified and categorized." Southern Poverty Law Center, March 18, 2020. https://www.splcenter.org/news/2020/03/18/methodology-how-hate-groups-are-identified-and-categorized

11. S. Noone. "Twitter suspends 70,000 accounts following US Capitol riots." News Nation, January 11, 2021. https://www.newsnationnow.com/us-news/dc-riots/twitter-suspends-70000-accounts-following-riot/

12. K. Gardner. "Social Media: Where Voices of Hate Find a Place to Preach." The Center for Public Integrity, August 30, 2018. https://publicintegrity.org/politics/social-media-where-voices-of-hate-find-a-place-to-preach/

13. I. Haimowitz. "No One is Immune: The Spread of QAnon through Social Media and the Pandemic." December 17, 2020. https://www.csis.org/blogs/technology-policy-blog/no-one-immune-spread-q-anon-through-social-media-and-pandemic

14. Ibid.

15. P.C. O'Brien. "Social Media History and Use." In *Social Media*, edited by K. Langmia et al., xviii–xix (New York, NY: University Press of America, 2014).

16. N. Usher. "The Appropriation/Amplification Model of Citizen Journalism." *Journalism Practice* (2016) http://dx.doi.org/10.1080/17512786.2016.1223552

17. D. L. Lasorsa, S. C. Lewis, and A. E. Holton. "Normalizing Twitter: Journalism Practice in an Emerging Communication Space." *Journalism Studies* 13 (2012): 19–36.

Chapter 2

1. A. Hermida. "From TV to Twitter: How Ambient News Became Ambient Journalism." *M/C Journal* 13: 2 (2010). https://doi.org/10.5204/mcj.220

2. D. Shedden. "Today in Media History: 2009 Hudson River crash-landing photo sent with Twitter." *Poynter*, January 15, 2015. https://www.poynter.org/reporting-editing/2015/today-in-media-history-2009-hudson-river-crash-landing-photo-sent-with-twitter/

3. S. Harlow. "Social Media and Social Movements: Facebook and an Online Guatemalan Justice Movement that Moved Offline." *New Media & Society* 14:2 (2012): 225–243.

4. Ibid.

5. P. N. Howard, A. Duffy, D. Freelon, M. M. Hussain, W. Mari, and M. Maziad. *Opening Closed Regimes: What Was the Role of Social Media During the Arab Spring?* Social Science Research Network (SSRN), 2011. http://ssrn.com/abstract=2595096

6. Ibid.

7. A. Hermida, S. C. Lewis, and R. Zamith. "Sourcing the Arab Spring: A Case Study of Andy Carvin's Sources on Twitter during the Tunisian and Egyptian Revolutions." *Journal of Computer-Mediated Communication* 19:3 (2014): 479–499.

8. K. M. DeLuca, S. Lawson, and Y. Sun. "Occupy Wall Street on the Public Screens of Social Media: The Many Framings of the Birth of a Protest Movement." *Communication, Culture & Critique* 5:4 (2012): 483–509.

9. R. Wang, W. Liu, and S. Gao. "Hashtags and Information Virality in Networked Social Movement." *Online Information Review* 40:7 (2016): 850–866.

10. K. Nahon and J. Hemsley. *Going Viral.* Cambridge, UK: Polity, 2013, 16.

11. Wang, Liu, and Gao. "Hashtags and Information Virality in Networked Social Movement."

12. S. Jackson. "#GirlsLikeUs: Trans advocacy and community building online." *New Media and Society* 20, No. 5 (2018): 1868–1888.

13. S. Liao. "'#IAmGay# What About You?': Storytelling, Discursive Politics, and the Affective Dimension of Social Media Activist against Censorship in China." *International Journal of Communication* 13 (2019): 2314–2333.

14. M. Li et al. "Twitter as a Tool for Social Movement: An Analysis of Feminist Activism on Social Media Communities." *Journal of Community Psychology* (2020). https://doi.org/10.1002/jcop.22324

15. C. Shirky. *Here Comes Everybody: The Power of Organizing Without Organizations.* New York, NY: The Penguin Press, 2008.

16. L. Rainie and B. Wellman. *Networked: The New Social Operating System.* Cambridge, MA: MIT Press, 2012.

17. C. Shirky. *Here Comes Everybody.*

18. Z. Tufekci. *Twitter and Tear Gas: The Power and Fragility of Networked Protest.* New Haven, CT: Yale University Press, 2017.

19. B. Zadrozny and B. Collins. "Videos, threats, but few signs protests have been stoked by 'outsider' extremist groups." *NBC News,* May 31, 2020. https://www.nbcnews.com/tech/security/videos-threats-few-signs-protests-have-been-stoked-outsider-extremist-n1220451

20. J. L. Blevins, J. J. Lee, E. E. McCabe, and E. Edgerton. "Tweeting for Social Justice in #Ferguson: Affective Discourse in Twitter Hashtags." *New Media & Society* 21:7 (2019): 1636–53. https://doi.org/10.1177/1461444819827030

21. K. Starbird. "The Surprising Nuance Behind the Russian Troll Strategy." *Medium,* October 20, 2018. https://medium.com/s/story/the-trolls-within-how-russian-information-operations-infiltrated-online-communities-691fb969b9e4

22. K. Starbird. "The Surprising Nuance Behind the Russian Troll Strategy." *Medium,* October 20, 2018. https://medium.com/s/story/the-trolls-within-how-russian-information-operations-infiltrated-online-communities-691fb969b9e4

23. C. Fuchs. *Culture and Economy in the Age of Social Media.* New York, NY: Routledge, 2015.

24. Z. Papacharissi. "Affective Publics and Structures of Storytelling: Sentiment, Events and Mediality." *Information, Communication & Society* 19 (2015): 307–324.

25. E.S. Herman and N. Chomsky. *Manufacturing Consent: The Political Economy of Mass Media* (with a new introduction by the authors, 2002 ed.). New York, NY: Pantheon Books, 1998, 2002.

Chapter 3

1. "Woman streams graphic video of boyfriend shot by police." *CNN*, July 7, 2016. http://www.cnn.com/videos/us/2016/07/07/graphic-video-minnesota-police -shooting-philando-castile-ryan-young-pkg-nd.cnn/video/playlists/philando -castile-shot-in-minnesota/.

2. J. L. Blevins, J. J. Lee, E. E. McCabe, and E. Edgerton. "Tweeting for Social Justice in #Ferguson: Affective Discourse in Twitter Hashtags." *New Media & Society* 21:7 (2019): 1636–1653. https://doi.org/10.1177/1461444819827030.

3. D. Freelon, C. D. McIlwain, and M. D. Clark. *Beyond the Hashtags: #Ferguson, #BlackLivesMatter, and the Online Struggle for Offline Justice.* Center for Media and Social Impact, School of Communication, American University, Washington, D.C., 2016, 9. https://cmsimpact.org/resource/beyond-hashtags-ferguson-black livesmatter-online-struggle-offline-justice/

4. S. J. Jackson and B. F. Welles. "Hijacking #myNYPD: Social Media Dissent and Networked Counterpublics." *Journal of Communication* 65:6 (2015): 932–52.

5. R. J. Gallagher, A. J. Reagan, C. M. Danforth, and P. S. Dodds. "Divergent Discourse Between Protests and Counter-protests: #BlackLivesMatter and #AllLivesMatter." *PLoS ONE* 13:4 (2018): e0195644. https://doi.org/10.1371/ journal.pone.0195644.

6. Ibid.

7. A. Olteanu, I. Weber, and D. Gatica-Perez. Characterizing the Demographics Behind the #BlackLivesMatter Movement. 2015. arXiv:1512.05671.

8. Freelon, McIlwain, and Clark. *Beyond the Hashtags*, p. 10.

9. Ibid.

10. Z. Papacharissi. "Affective Publics and Structures of Storytelling: Sentiment, Events and Mediality." *Information, Communication & Society* 19 (2015): 309.

11. Freelon, McIlwain, and Clark. *Beyond the Hashtags*, p. 19.

12. R. M. Entman. "Framing: Toward Clarification of a Fractured Paradigm." *Journal of Communication* 43:4 (1993): 51–58.

13. J. L. Blevins, J. J. Lee, E. E. McCabe, and E. Edgerton. "Tweeting for Social Justice in #Ferguson: Affective Discourse in Twitter Hashtags." *New Media & Society* 21:7 (2019): 1636–1653. https://doi.org/10.1177/1461444819827030.

14. A. Goldstein. "Palestinian and Ferguson Protestors Link Arms Via Social Media." *Yes! Magazine*, August 15, 2014. http://www.yesmagazine.org/peace-justice/palest inians-and-ferguson-protesters-link-arms-via-social-media.

15. D. McCormack. "St. Louis Rams Players Stage 'Hands Up, Don't Shoot' Protest at NFL Game in Solidarity with Ferguson Protestors." *Daily Mail* (United Kingdom), November 30, 2014. http://www.dailymail.co.uk/news/article-2855253/Five-St -Louis-Rams-players-field-arms-raised-hands-don-t-shot-gesture-solidarity -Ferguson-protesters.html.

16. Z. Papacharissi. "Affective Publics and Structures of Storytelling: Sentiment, Events and Mediality." *Information, Communication & Society* 19 (2015): 307–324.

17. Ibid.

18. J. L. Blevins. "Social Media Mobbing Diminishes the Quality of Public Discourse." The Cincinnati Project, August 28, 2016. https://thecincyproject.org/2016/ 08/28/social-media-mobbing-diminishes-the-quality-of-public-discourse/.

Chapter 4

1. J. L. Blevins. "Social Media and Social Justice Movements after the Diminution of Black-Owned Media in the United States." In *Media Across the African Diaspora: Content, Audiences, and Global Influence*, edited by O. O. Banjo, 191–203. New York, NY: Routledge, 2019; J. L. Blevins and K. Martinez. "A Political-Economic History of FCC Policy on Minority Broadcast Ownership." *The Communication Review* 13: 3 (2010): 216–238.

2. R. R. Mourao, D. K. Kilgo, and G. Sylvie. "Framing Ferguson: The Interplay of Advocacy and Journalistic Frames in Local and National Newspaper Coverage of Michael Brown." *Journalism* (2018). https://doi.org/10.1177/1464884918778722

3. Ibid.

4. Ibid.

5. A. Carvin. *Distant Witness: Social Media and the Arab Spring and a Journalism Revolution.* New York, NY: CUNY Journalism Press, 2012.

6. Fox19 Digital Staff. "Bigger than a moment: Documenting the outcry of our city." *FOX19, WXIX-TV*, October 27, 2020. https://www.fox19.com/2020/10/27/bigger -than-moment-documenting-outcry-our-city/

7. Z. Papacharissi. "Affective Publics and Structures of Storytelling: Sentiment, Events and Mediality." *Information, Communication & Society* 19 (2015): 309.

8. Freelon, McIlwain, and Clark. *Beyond the Hashtags*, p. 19.

9. Christina Brown. Private interview conducted by Jeffrey Layne Blevins at Café DeSales in Cincinnati, March 16, 2017.

10. Mona Jenkins. Private interview conducted by Jeffrey Layne Blevins at Café DeSales in Cincinnati, March 16, 2017.

11. Brown interview.

12. Jenkins interview.

13. Brown interview.

14. Ibid.

15. Ibid.

16. Jenkins interview.

17. Brown interview.

18. I. Jackson. March 30, 2018. "Black Lives Matter Cincinnati changes its name, issues scathing critique of national BLM network." *Black Youth Project*. http://blackyouthproject.com/black-lives-matter-cincinnati-changes-its-name-issues-scathing-critique-of-national-blm/

19. D. R. Stewart and J. Littau. "Up, Periscope: Mobile Streaming Video Technologies, Privacy in Public, and the Right to Record." *Journalism & Mass Communication Quarterly* 93:2 (2016): 312–31.

20. J. Breitbart. "A Victory for Digital Justice." In *Strategies for Media Reform: International Perspectives*, edited by D. Freedman, J. A. Obar, C. Martens, and R. W. McChesney, 107–14. New York, NY: Fordham University Press, 2016.

21. J. Eggerton. "Update: House OK's Amendment to Defund FCC Chief Diversity Officer." *Broadcasting & Cable*, February 17, 2011. http://www.broadcastingcable.com/news/news-articles/update-house-oks-amendment-defund-fcc-chief-diversity-officer/111640

22. J. Breitbart. "A Victory for Digital Justice." In *Strategies for Media Reform: International Perspectives*, edited by D. Freedman, J. A. Obar, C. Martens, and R. W. McChesney, 107–14. New York, NY: Fordham University Press, 2016, 113.

23. D. Freedman and J. A. Obar. "Media Reform: An Overview." In *Strategies for Media Reform: International Perspectives*, edited by D. Freedman, J. A. Obar, C. Martens, and R. W. McChesney. New York: Fordham University Press, 2016, 7.

24. Ibid., 3.

25. J. L. Blevins. "Panoptic Missorts and the Hegemony of U.S. Data Privacy Policy." *Political Economy of Communication*, 4:2 (2016): 26.

26. D. Freedman and J. A. Obar. "Media Reform: An Overview." In *Strategies for Media Reform: International Perspectives*, edited by D. Freedman, J. A. Obar, C. Martens, and R. W. McChesney. New York: Fordham University Press, 2016, 5.

Chapter 5

1. M. Anderson. "Social Media Conversations about Race: How Social Media Users See, Share, and Discuss Race and the Rise of Hashtags Like #BlackLivesMatter." Pew Research Center, Washington, D.C. 2016. http://www.pewinternet.org/2016/08/15/social-media-conversations-about-race/

2. J. L. Blevins. "Social Media Mobbing Diminishes the Quality of Public Discourse." The Cincinnati Project, August 28, 2016. https://thecincyproject.org/2016/08/28/social-media-mobbing-diminishes-the-quality-of-public-discourse/.

3. L. Fisher and B. McBride. "'Ghostbusters' Star Leslie Jones Quites Twitter After Online Harassment." ABC News, July 20, 2016. https://abcnews.go.com/Entertainment/ghostbusters-star-leslie-jones-quits-twitter-online-harassment/story?id=40698459

4. M. Chan. "Cincinnati Zoo Deactivates Twitter Account Amid Flood of Harambe Mentions." Time, August 23, 2016. http://time.com/4462675/cincinnati-zoo-deactivates-twitter-harambe/.

5. E. Noelle-Neumann. "The Spiral of Silence: A Theory of Public Opinion." Journal of Communication 24 (1974): 43–51 for an explication of "spiral of silence" theory.

6. Brittany Bibb. Private interview conducted by Jeffrey Layne Blevins at the African American Cultural Resource Center on the campus of the University of Cincinnati, March 28, 2019.

7. Ibid.

8. Ibid.

9. Bibb discusses in further detail how The Irate 8 came together in the aftermath of the Sam DuBose killing, as well as its social media campaign in her Soundcloud archive (see https://soundcloud.com/whatis_tcp/sets/archiving-activism-brittany).

10. M. McPhate. "Gorilla Killed After Child Enters Enclosure at Cincinnati Zoo." The New York Times, May 20, 2016. https://www.nytimes.com/2016/05/30/us/gorilla-killed-after-child-enters-enclosure-at-cincinnati-zoo.html

11. J. L. Blevins. "Social Media Disparity in #JusticeForHarambe and #DisneyGatorAttack." The Cincinnati Herald (Cincinnati, OH), July 9–15, 2016, B1, B3.

12. E. C. McLaughlin, J. Berlinger, A. Fantz, and S. Almasy. "Disney Gator Attack: 2-year-old Boy Found Dead." CNN, June 16, 2016. https://www.cnn.com/2016/06/15/us/alligator-attacks-child-disney-florida/index.html

13. R. Ellis, A. Fantz, F. Karimi, and E. C. McLaughlin. "Orlando Shooting: 49 Killed, Shooter Pledged ISIS Allegiance." CNN, June 13, 2016. https://www.cnn.com/2016/06/12/us/orlando-nightclub-shooting/index.html

14. S. Denson. "Ohio Zoo: Mom Dangling Toddler over Cheetah Pit when He Fell." WKRN.com, April 12, 2015. https://www.wkrn.com/news/ohio-zoo-mom -dangling-toddler-over-cheetah-pit-when-he-fell/1089250596

15. B. G. Johnson. "The Heckler's Veto: Using First Amendment Theory and Jurisprudence to Understand Current Audience Reactions Against Controversial Speech." *Communication Law & Policy* 21: 2 (2016): 215.

16. B. G. Johnson. "The Heckler's Veto," 219.

17. Ibid.

18. P. M. Napoli. *Audience Evolution: New Technologies and Transformation of Media Audiences.* New York, NY: Columbia University Press, 2010, 5.

19. B. G. Johnson. "The Heckler's Veto," 219.

Chapter 6

1. S. Wojcik, S. Messing, A. Smith, L. Rainie, and P. Hitlin. "Bots in the Twittersphere: An estimated two-thirds of tweeted links to popular websites are posted by automated accounts—not human beings." Pew Research Center, April 9, 2018. Retrieved February 10, 2019. http://www.pewinternet.org/2018/04/09/bots-in -the-twittersphere/

2. See W. Liu, A. Sidhu, A. M. Beacom, and T. W. Valente. "Social Network Theory." In *The International Encyclopedia of Media Effects,* edited by P. Rossler, C. A. Hoffner and L. van Zoonen, 1–12. Hoboken, NJ: John Wiley & Sons, Inc.

Chapter 7

1. M. Anderson. "Social Media Conversations About Race: How Social Media Users See, Share, and Discuss Race and the Rise of Hashtags Like #BlackLivesMatter." Pew Research Center, Washington D.C., 2016. http://www.pewinternet.org/ 2016/08/15/social-media-conversations-about-race/

2. C. Silverman and L. Alexander. "How Teens In The Balkans are Duping Trump Supporters With Fake News." *Buzzfeed,* November 3, 2016. https://www.buzz-feednews.com/article/craigsilverman/how-macedonia-became-a-global-hub-for -pro-trump-misinfo

3. U.S. House of Representatives, Permanent Select Committee on Intelligence Social Media, 2017. Retrieved February 10, 2019. https://democratsintelligence .house.gov/facebook-ads/social-media-advertisements.htm

4. G. Orwell. *1984.* Secker & Warburg: London, UK: Secker & Warburg, 1949.

5. D. O'Sullivan. "The Biggest Black Lives Matter Page on Facebook Is Fake." *CNN Business,* April 9, 2018. Retrieved February 10, 2019. http://money.cnn .com/2018/04/09/technology/fake-black-lives-matter-facebook-page/index.html

Chapter 8

1. C. Fuchs. *Culture and Economy in the Age of Social Media.* New York, NY: Routledge, 2015; Z. Papacharissi. "Affective Publics and Structures of Storytelling: Sentiment, Events and Mediality." *Information, Communication & Society* 19 (2015): 307–24.

2. E. S. Herman and N. Chomsky. *Manufacturing Consent: The Political Economy of Mass Media* (with a new introduction by the authors, 2002 ed.). New York, NY: Pantheon Books, 1988; 2002. In this analysis we reference Herman and Chomsky's 1988 book, *Manufacturing Consent: The Political Economy of Mass Media*, which was reprinted in 2002 with a new introduction by the authors. When citing material from the new introduction, we reference "Herman and Chomsky, 2002," while content from their original analysis is cited as "Herman and Chomsky, 1988."

3. L. McIntyre. *Post-Truth*. Cambridge, MA: MIT Press, 2018.

4. J. L. Blevins, E. Edgerton, D. P. Jason, and J. J. Lee. "Shouting into the wind: Medical Science v. 'B.S.' in the Twitter Maelstrom of Politics and Misinformation About Hydroxychloroquine." *Social Media + Society* 7:2 (2021): 1–14.

5. Herman and Chomsky, *Manufacturing Consent*, 1988 edition.

6. R. W. McChesney. *The Political Economy of Media: Enduring Issues, Emerging Dilemmas*. New York, NY: Monthly Review Press, 2008:12.

7. E. Meehan, V. Mosco, and J. Wasko. 1993. "Rethinking Political Economy: Change and Continuity." *Journal of Communication* 43(4): 105–16.

8. W. Lippmann. *Public Opinion* (reprint). London: Allen & Unwin, 1921; 1932; H. Laswell. *Propaganda Technique in the World War* (reprint). New York, NY: Peter Smith, 1927; 1938; Herman and Chomsky (1988) adapted the phrase "manufacturing consent" from Lippmann's (1921; 1932) book, *Public Opinion*.

9. Herman and Chomsky. *Manufacturing Consent*, 1988 edition, pp. 3–14.

10. Quoted in Herman and Chomsky, *Manufacturing Consent*. See J. Curran and J. Seaton, *Power Without Responsibility*. London: Fontana, 1981, p. 31 for original quote.

11. Herman and Chomsky, *Manufacturing Consent*, pp. 14–18.

12. Herman and Chomsky, *Manufacturing Consent*, p. 14.

13. Ibid.

14. Herman and Chomsky, *Manufacturing Consent*, p. 19.

15. Herman and Chomsky, *Manufacturing Consent*, p. 23.

16. Herman and Chomsky, *Manufacturing Consent*, p. 26.

17. Herman and Chomsky, *Manufacturing Consent*, p. 28.

18. Herman and Chomsky, *Manufacturing Consent*, p. 29.

19. Ibid.

20. Ibid.

21. Herman and Chomsky, *Manufacturing Consent,* 2002 edition, p. xv.

22. Herman and Chomsky, *Manufacturing Consent* 2002 edition, p. xvi.

23. Ibid.

24. Herman and Chomsky, *Manufacturing Consent,* 2002 edition, p. xii.

25. Herman and Chomsky, *Manufacturing Consent,* 2002 edition, p. xvi; see also Blevins, "Battle of the On-line Brans," 2004; Aufderheide, "Competition and Commons," 2006; Blevins, "Source Diversity After the Telecommunications Act of 1996," 2002; McChesney, "The Internet and U.S. Communication," 1996.

26. Herman and Chomsky, *Manufacturing Consent.* 2002 edition, p. xix.

27. Herman and Chomsky, *Manufacturing Consent.* 1988 edition, p. xi.

28. T. F. Corrigan. "Making Implicit Methods Explicit: Trade Press Analysis in the Political Economy of Communication." *International Journal of Communication* 12 (2018): 2753–75.

29. Ibid.

30. "Two Popular Conservative Twitter Personalities Were Just Outed as Russian Trolls: Jenna Abrams and Pamela Moore Were Followed by Tens of Thousands, Including Members of Trump's Campaign," *Philadelphia Inquirer,* 2017, Nov. 3. https://www.inquirer.com/philly/news/politics/presidential/russia-fake-twitter -facebook-posts-accounts-trump-election-jenna-abrams-20171103.html

31. S. C. Woolley and D. Guilbeault. "Computational Propaganda in the United States of America: Manufacturing Consensus Online." In *Project on Computational Propaganda,* edited by S. Woolley and P. N. Howard. Oxford Internet Institute, Oxford, England. http://blogs.oii.ox.ac.uk/politicalbots/wp-content/uploads/ sites/89/2017/06/Comprop-USA.pdf

32. M. E. McCombs and D. L. Shaw. "The Agenda-Setting Function of Mass Media." *Public Opinion Quarterly* 36:2 (1972): 176–87; B. Heath, M. Wynn, and J. Guynn. "How a lie about George Soros and the migrant caravan multiplied online: USA TODAY followed the rapid spread of a social media conspiracy theory about George Soros and migrants that grew from obscurity to political mainstream." *USA Today,* October 31, 2018. https://www.usatoday.com/in-depth/ news/nation/2018/10/31/george-soros-and-migrant-caravan-how-lie-multiplied -online/1824633002/.

33. C. Silverman. "This Analysis Shows How Viral Fake Election News Stories Outperformed Read News on Facebook." *Buzzfeed,* November 16, 2016. Retrieved July 28, 2018. https://www.buzzfeednews.com/article/craigsilverman/viral-fake -election-news-outperformed-real-news-on-facebook.

34. Dayden, D. "How Twitter Secretly Benefits from Bots and Fake Accounts." *The Intercept*, 2017, Nov. 6. https://theintercept.com/2017/11/06/how-twitter-secretly -benefits-from-bots-and-fake-accounts/

35. Isaac, M. and D. Wakabayashi. "Russian Influence Reached 126 Million Through Facebook Alone." *The New York Times*, October 30, 2017. Retrieved July 28, 2018 from https://www.nytimes.com/2017/10/30/technology/facebook-google-russia .html

36. Herman and Chomsky, *Manufacturing Consent,* 1988 edition, p. xii.

37. Herman and Chomsky, *Manufacturing Consent,* 2002 edition, p. xii.

38. Herman and Chomsky, *Manufacturing Consent,*1988 edition.

39. Keller, M. H. "The Business of Serving Up YouTube Views." *The New York Times, August 12, 2018,* p. 1.

40. Ibid. p. 18.

41. Herman and Chomsky, *Manufacturing Consent* 1988 edition.

42. M. Hindmanand V. Barash. *Disinformation, "Fake News" and Influence Campaigns on Twitter.* The Knight Foundation. Retrieved October 8, 2018. https://kf-site -production.s3.amazonaws.com/media_elements/files/000/000/238/original/KF -DisinformationReport-final2.pdf

43. NBC News published a subset of about 200,000 of the IRA-manufactured tweets after they were revealed in a grand jury indictment (see https://www.justice.gov/ file/1035477/download); and FiveThirtyEight completed a larger examination of approximately 3 million of those tweets later in 2018 based on a data set compiled by Clemson University researchers Darren Linvill and Patrick Warren (see https://github.com/fivethirtyeight/russian-troll-tweets/).

44. Roeder, O. "Why We're Sharing 3 Million Russian Troll Tweets." FiveThirtyEight, July 31, 2018. https://fivethirtyeight.com/features/why-were-sharing-3-million -russian-troll-tweets/

45. D. L. Linvill and P. L. Warren. (2018). "Troll Factories: The Internet Research Agency and State-Sponsored Agenda Building." Working paper. http://pwarren .people.clemson.edu/Linvill_Warren_TrollFactory.pdf

46. C. Timber. "The Strange Birth, Death and Rebirth of Russian Troll Account 'AllForUSA.'" *The Washington Post*, August 7, 2019, A4.

47. Herman and Chomsky, *Manufacturing Consent,* 1988 edition.

48. J. Diamond. "Trump Launches All-out Attack on the Press." *CNN*, June 1, 2016. https://www.cnn.com/2016/05/31/politics/donald-trump-veterans-announce ment/index.html

49. M. Isaac and J. Nicas. "Facebook Cuts Ties with Washington Firm That Sought to Discredit Social Network's Critics." *The New York Times*, November 15, 2018.

https://www.nytimes.com/2018/11/15/technology/facebook-definers-soros.html
?action=click&module=Top%20Stories&pgtype=Homepage

50. C. Kang, M. Rosenberg, and M. Issac. "Mark Zuckerberg Defends Facebook as
     Furor Over Its Tactics Grows." *The New York Times*, November 15, 2018. https://
     www.nytimes.com/2018/11/15/technology/zuckerberg-facebook-sandberg
     -tactics.html

51. D. Stanglin. "Trump, via Twitter, Says Social Media Discriminates Against GOP,
     Conservative Voices." *USA Today*, August 18, 2018. https://www.usatoday.com/
     story/news/2018/08/18/trump-says-social-media-discriminates-against-gop
     -conservatives/1030478002/

52. D. Kellner. *Grand Theft 2000: Media Spectacle and a Stolen Election*. New York, NY:
     Rowman & Littlefield, 2001, 140.

53. (U.S. Const., Amend. I)

54. S. Robinson. "Journalism as Process: The Organizational Implications of
     Participatory Online News." *Journalism & Communication Monographs* 13:3 (2011):
     202.

55. S. Wineburg, S. McGrew., J. Breakstone, and T. Ortega. *Evaluating Information:
     The Cornerstone of Civic Online Reasoning*. Stanford Digital Repository, 2016.
     https://purl.stanford.edu/fv751yt5934

56. A. J. Head, J. Wihbey, P. T. Metaxas, M. MacMillan, and D. Cohen. *How Students
     Engage with News: Five Takeaways for Educators, Journalists and Librarians*. Knight
     Foundation, Project Information Literacy, October 16, 2018. http://www
     .projectinfolit.org/uploads/2/7/5/4/27541717/newsreport.pdf

57. Herman and Chomsky, *Manufacturing Consent*, 1988 edition, pp. 1xii-1xiii.

58. G. Marcus and E. Davis. "A.I. Won't Fix Fake News." *The New York Times*,
     October 21, 2018, SR 6.

59. J. L. Blevins. "Panoptic Missorts and the Hegemony of U.S. Data Privacy Policy."
     The Political Economy of Communication 4:2 (2016):18-33.

60. D. O'Sullivan. "The Biggest Black Lives Matter Page on Facebook is Fake."
     CNN Business, April 9, 2018. Retrieved February 10, 2019. http://money.cnn
     .com/2018/04/09/technology/fake-black-lives-matter-facebook-page/index.html

61. S. Rossman, M. Wynn, J. Guynn, and B. Heath. "How a few shady social media
     posts fed a viral firestorm over Covington Catholic (and why it will happen
     again)." *USA Today*, Feb. 19, 2019. https://www.usatoday.com/story/news/
     investigations/2019/02/19/covington-catholic-outrage-spread-shady-facebook
     -and-twitter-posts/2667213002/

62. B. Zadrozny and B. Collins. "Videos, threats, but few signs protests have been
     stoked by 'outsider' extremist groups." *NBC News*, May 31, 2020. https://www

.nbcnews.com/tech/security/videos-threats-few-signs-protests-have-been-stoked
-outsider-extremist-n1220451

63. S. Rossman, M. Wynn, J. Guynn, and B. Heath. "How a few shady social media posts fed a viral firestorm over Covington Catholic (and why it will happen again)." *USA Today*, Feb. 19, 2019. https://www.usatoday.com/story/news/ investigations/2019/02/19/covington-catholic-outrage-spread-shady-facebook -and-twitter-posts/2667213002/

64. Ibid.

Chapter 9

1. S. Manuel. "Ga. protests lead to arrests of vigilantes in Arbery killing." *The Militant* 84:22, June 8, 2020. https://themilitant.com/2020/05/30/ga-protests -lead-to-arrests-of-vigilantes-in-arbery-killing/

2. P. Martinez. "Louisville police chief fired after fatal shooting of black business owner." *CBS News*, June 7, 2020. https://www.cbsnews.com/news/steve-conrad -louisville-police-chief-fired-protest-shooting-death/

3. A. Horton. "Hundreds of counter-protesters confront Black Lives Matter rally in Ohio." *The Guardian*, June 18, 2020. https://www.theguardian.com/us -news/2020/jun/18/hundreds-armed-counter-protesters-confront-black-lives -matter-event-bethel-ohio

4. J. L. Blevins, J. J. Lee, E. E. McCabe, and E. Edgerton. "Tweeting for Social Justice in #Ferguson: Affective Discourse in Twitter Hashtags." *New Media & Society* 21: 7 (2019): 1636–53. https://doi.org/10.1177/1461444819827030. See especially pp. 1642–44.

5. Ibid.

6. D. M. Owens. "#SayHerName: Breonna Taylor and hundreds of Black women have died at the hands of police. The movement to say their names is growing." *USA Today*, March 11, 2021. https://www.usatoday.com/in-depth/ news/investigations/2021/03/11/sayhername-movement-black-women-police -violence/6921197002/

7. J. Bates. "Indianapolis Police Officer Shoots Man in Livestreamed Killing. Here's What to Know." *Time*, May 7, 2020. https://time.com/5833625/indianapolis -police-shooting-sean-reed/

8. See African American Policy Forum, https://www.aapf.org/sayhername; and D. M. Owens. "#SayHerName."

Chapter 10

1. J. Mahone and P. Napoli. "Hundreds of hyperpartisan sites are masquerading as local news. This map shows if there's one near you." *Nieman Lab*, July 13, 2020. https://www.niemanlab.org/2020/07/hundreds-of-hyperpartisan-sites-are-masquerading-as-local-news-this-map-shows-if-theres-one-near-you/

2. P. Bengani. "Hundreds of 'pink slime' local news outlets are distributing algorithmic stories and conservative talking points." *Columbia Journalism Review*, December 18, 2019. https://www.cjr.org/tow_center_reports/hundreds-of-pink-slime-local-news-outlets-are-distributing-algorithmic-stories-conservative-talking-points.php

3. A. J. Stewart, M. Mosleh, M. Diakonova, A. A. Arechar, D. G. Rand, and J. B. Plotkin. "Information Gerrymandering and Undemocratic Decisions." *Nature* 573 (2019): 117–21.

4. C. Ward, K. Polglase, S. Shukla, G. Mezzofiore, and T. Lister. "Russian election meddling is back—via Ghana and Nigeria—and in your feeds." *CNN*, April 11, 2020. https://www.cnn.com/2020/03/12/world/russia-ghana-troll-farms-2020-ward/index.html.

5. Ibid.

6. B. Collins, B. Zadrozny, and E. Saliba. "White nationalist group posing as antifa called for violence on Twitter: Other misinformation and misleading claims spread across Twitter on Sunday night and into Monday related to the protests." *NBC News*, June 1, 2020. https://www.nbcnews.com/tech/security/twitter-takes-down-washington-protest-disinformation-bot-behavior-n1221456

7. B. Zadrozny and B. Collins. "Videos, threats, but few signs protests have been stoked by 'outsider' extremist groups." *NBC News*, May 31, 2020. https://www.nbcnews.com/tech/security/videos-threats-few-signs-protests-have-been-stoked-outsider-extremist-n1220451

8. A. Madhani and J. Colvin. "Farewell, @realDonaldTrump: Looking back at the Twitter account's provocative history." *USA Today*, Jan. 9, 2021. https://amp.usatoday.com/amp/6607069002?__twitter_impression=true

9. B. Naylor and R. Lucas. "Wray Stresses Role of Right-Wing Extremism in Hearing about Jan. 6 Riot." *NPR*, March 2, 2021. https://www.npr.org/2021/03/02/972539274/fbi-director-wray-testifies-before-congress-for-1st-time-since-capitol-attack

10. E. Dwoskin and C. Timberg. "Misinformation dropped dramatically the week after Twitter banned Trump and some allies: Zignal Labs charts 73 percent decline on Twitter and beyond following historic action against the president."

The Washington Post, January 16, 2021. https://www.washingtonpost.com/tech nology/2021/01/16/misinformation-trump-twitter/

11. J. Guynn. "Twitter suspends 70,000 QAnon accounts in massive purge after deadly Capitol siege, Trump ban." *USA Today*, January 11. 2021. https://www .usatoday.com/story/tech/2021/01/11/twitter-purge-qanon-accounts-permanent -suspension-trump-capitol-riots/6633629002/

12. J. Guynn. "Facebook While Black: Users Call it Getting 'Zucked,' Say Talking about Racism is Censored as hate Speech." *USA Today*, April 24, 2019. https:// www.usatoday.com/story/news/2019/04/24/facebook-while-black-zucked-users -say-they-get-blocked-racism-discussion/2859593002/

13. J. Blevins. "Panoptic Missorts and the Hegemony of U.S. Data Privacy Policy." *Political Economy of Communication* 4:2 (2016): 18–33.

14. A. Mitchell, J. Gottfried, G. Stocking, M. Walker, and S. Feldi. "Many Americans Say Made-Up News Is a Critical Problem That Needs to Be Fixed." Pew Research Center, June 5, 2019. https://www.journalism.org/2019/06/05/many-americans -say-made-up-news-is-a-critical-problem-that-needs-to-be-fixed/

15. See https://firstdraftnews.org/latest/author/cwardle/

16. See https://www.theguardian.com/uk/interactive/2011/dec/07/london-riots-twitter

17. R. J. Shiller. *Narrative Economics*. Princeton, NJ: Princeton University Press, 2019.

18. See, for example, Kreiss's 2016 analysis of how candidates Obama and Mitt Romney used Twitter during the 2012 electoral cycle.

19. B. O'Malley. "Antonio French's tweets chronicled Ferguson protests." *St. Louis Post-Dispatch* (St. Louis, MO), August 29. 2014. https://www.stltoday.com/ news/multimedia/special/antonio-frenchs-tweets-chronicled-ferguson-protests/ article_ffabdcf0-405c-5ce3-82bb-e32560915ed4.html; and L. Mandaro. "300 Ferguson tweets: A day's work for Antonio French." *USA Today*, August 25, 2014. https://www.usatoday.com/story/news/nation-now/2014/08/25/antonio-french -twitter-ferguson/14457633/

20. J. Peters. "More than 20 months after Ferguson, Ryan Reilly and Wesley Lowery are still facing charges in St. Louis County." *Columbia Journalism Review*, April 19, 2016. https://www.cjr.org/united_states_project/ryan_reilly_wesley_lowery_ferg uson_charges.php

21. J. McEvoy. "Jury Acquits Iowa Reporter Arrested While Covering Black Lives Matter Protest." *Forbes*, March 10, 2021. https://www.forbes.com/sites/jemima mcevoy/2021/03/10/jury-acquits-iowa-reporter-arrested-while-covering-black -lives-matter-protests/?sh=6b6778664ef4

References

"2017–08-partisan-sites-and-facebook-pages." 2017. *Buzzfeed*. http://bit.ly/Partisan
  Data

American Recovery and Reinvestment Act of 2009. Pub. L. No. 111–5, 123 Stat. 115.

Anderson, M. 2016. "Social Media Conversations about Race: How Social Media Users
  See, Share and Discuss Race and the Rise of Hashtags Like #BlackLivesMatter."
  Pew Research Center, Washington, D.C. http://www.pewinternet.org/2016/08/15/
  social-media-conversations-about-race/

Aufderheide, P. 2006. "Competition and Commons: The Public Interest In and After
  the AOL-Time Warner Merger." *Journal of Broadcasting & Electronic Media* 46 (1):
  531–51.

Bagdikian, B. 1987. *The Media Monopoly*, 2nd ed. Boston, MA: Beacon Press.

Bates, J. 2020. "Indianapolis Police Officer Shoots Man in Livestreamed Killing. Here's
  What to Know." *Time*, May 7. https://time.com/5833625/indianapolis-police
  -shooting-sean-reed/

Bengani, P. 2019. "Hundreds of 'Pink Slime' Local News Outlets Are Distributing
  Algorithmic Stories and Conservative Talking Points." *Columbia Journalism
  Review*, December 18. https://www.cjr.org/tow_center_reports/hundreds-of-pink
  -slime-local-news-outlets-are-distributing-algorithmic-stories-conservative-talk
  ing-points.php

Berlet, C. 2001. "When Hate Went Online." Paper presented to the Northeast
  Sociological Association, Spring Conference at Sacred Heart University in
  Fairfield, CT, April 28. http://citeseerx.ist.psu.edu/viewdoc/download?doi=10.1.1
  .552.239&rep=rep1&type=pdf

Bibb, Brittany. 2019. Private interview conducted by Jeffrey Layne Blevins at the
  African American Cultural Resource Center on the campus of the University of
  Cincinnati, March 28, 2019.

Blevins, J. L. 2001. "Counter-Hegemonic Media: Can Cyberspace Resist Corporate
  Colonization?" In *Cyberimperialism? Global Relations in the New Electronic Frontier*,
  edited by B. Ebo, 139–51. Westport, CT: Praeger.

Blevins, J. L. 2002. "Source Diversity After the Telecommunications Act of 1996: Media Oligarchs Begin to Colonize Cyberspace." *Television & New Media* 3(1): 95–112.

———. 2004. "Battle of the On-Line Brands: Disney Loses Internet Portal War." *Television & New Media* 5 (3): 247–71.

———. 2014. "Social Media Empowered in #Ferguson." *The Cincinnati Enquirer* (Cincinnati, OH), September 27, A15.

———. 2016. "Social Media Disparity in #JusticeForHarambe and #DisneyGatorAttack." *The Cincinnati Herald* (Cincinnati, OH), July 9–15, B1, B3.

———. 2016. "Social Media Mobbing Diminishes the Quality of Public Discourse." The Cincinnati Project, August 28. https://thecincyproject.org/2016/08/28/social-media-mobbing-diminishes-the-quality-of-public-discourse/.

———. 2016. "Panoptic Missorts and the Hegemony of U.S. Data Privacy Policy." *Political Economy of Communication* 4(2): 18–33.

———. 2019. "Social Media and Social Justice Movements after the Diminution of Black-Owned Media in the United States." In *Media Across the African Diaspora: Content, Audiences, and Global Influence*, edited by O. O. Banjo, 191–203. New York, NY: Routledge.

Blevins, J. L., and Martinez, K. 2010. "A Political-Economic History of FCC Policy on Minority Broadcast Ownership." *The Communication Review* 13(3): 216–38.

Blevins, J. L., J. J. Lee, E. E. McCabe, and E. Edgerton. 2019. "Tweeting for Social Justice in #Ferguson: Affective Discourse in Twitter Hashtags." *New Media & Society* 21(7): 1636–53. https://doi.org/10.1177/1461444819827030

Blevins, J. L., E. Edgerton, D. P. Jason, and J. J. Lee. 2021. "Shouting into the Wind: Medical Science v. 'B.S.' in the Twitter Maelstrom of Politics and Misinformation about Hydroxychloroquine." *Social Media + Society* 7 (2): 1–14. https://doi.org/10.1177/20563051211024977

Bonazzo, J. 2017. "Facebook Removes White Nationalist Group Pages After Charlottesville Attack: Twitter and Reddit Face Scrutiny for Allowing Hate Speech." *The Observer*, August 16. https://observer.com/2017/08/charlottesville-facebook-removes-racist-pages/

Boyd, D. M. and N. B. Ellison. 2007. "Social Network Sites: Definition, History, and Scholarship." *Journal of Computer-Mediated Communication* 13(1): 210–30.

Breitbart, J. 2016. "A Victory for Digital Justice." In *Strategies for Media Reform: International Perspectives*, edited by D. Freedman, J. A. Obar, C. Martens, and R. W. McChesney, 107–14. New York, NY: Fordham University Press.

Brown, Christina. 2017. Private interview conducted by Jeffrey Layne Blevins at Café DeSales in Cincinnati, OH, March 16.

Carvin, A. 2012. *Distant Witness: Social Media and the Arab Spring and a Journalism Revolution.* New York, NY: CUNY Journalism Press.

Chan, M. "Cincinnati Zoo Deactivates Twitter Account Amid Flood of Harambe Mentions." *Time*, August 23, 2016. http://time.com/4462675/cincinnati-zoo -deactivates-twitter-harambe/

Collins, B., B. Zadrozny, and E. Saliba. 2020. "White Nationalist Group Posing as Antifa Called for Violence on Twitter: Other Misinformation and Misleading Claims Spread across Twitter on Sunday Night and into Monday Related to the Protests." *NBC News*, June 1. https://www.nbcnews.com/tech/security/twitter -takes-down-washington-protest-disinformation-bot-behavior-n1221456

Communications Decency Act of 1996, Pub. L. No. 104–104, 110 Stat. 56.

Corrigan, T. F. 2018. "Making Implicit Methods Explicit: Trade Press Analysis in the Political Economy of Communication." *International Journal of Communication* 12: 2751–72.

Crump, J. 2021. "The Case Against Trump: A Look at His Tweets from January 6th." *The Independent*, February 12. https://www.independent.co.uk/news/world/ americas/us-politics/trump-tweets-jan-6-impeachment-evidence-b1801715.html

Curran, J. and J. Seaton. 1981. *Power Without Responsibility.* London, UK: Fontana.

Dayen, D. 2017. "How Twitter Secretly Benefits from Bots and Fake Accounts." *The Intercept*, November 6. https://theintercept.com/2017/11/06/how-twitter-secretly -benefits-from-bots-and-fake-accounts/.

DeLuca, K. M., S. Lawson, and Y. Sun. 2012. "Occupy Wall Street on the Public Screens of Social Media: The Many Framings of the Birth of a Protest Movement." *Communication, Culture & Critique* 5(4): 483–509.

Denson, S. 2015. "Ohio Zoo: Mom Dangling Toddler over Cheetah Pit When He Fell." *WKRN.com*, April 12. https://www.wkrn.com/news/ohio-zoo-mom-dangling -toddler-over-cheetah-pit-when-he-fell/1089250596

Diamond, J. 2016. "Trump Launches All-out Attack on the Press." *CNN*, June 1. https://www.cnn.com/2016/05/31/politics/donald-trump-veterans-announce ment/index.html

Dwoskin, E. and C. Timberg. 2021. "Misinformation Dropped Dramatically the Week after Twitter Banned Trump and Some Allies: Zignal Labs Charts 73 percent Decline on Twitter and Beyond Following Fistoric Action Against the President." *The Washington Post*, January 16. https://www.washingtonpost.com/technology/ 2021/01/16/misinformation-trump-twitter/

Eggerton, J. 2011. "Update: House OK's Amendment to Defund FCC Chief Diversity Officer." *Broadcasting & Cable*, February 17. http://www.broadcastingcable.com/ news/news-articles/update-house-oks-amendment-defund-fcc-chief-diversity -officer/111640

Ellis, R., A. Fantz, F. Karimi, and E. C. McLaughlin. 2016. "Orlando Shooting: 49 Killed, Shooter Pledged ISIS Allegiance." *CNN*, June 13. https://www.cnn .com/2016/06/12/us/orlando-nightclub-shooting/index.html

Entman, R. M. 1993. "Framing: Toward Clarification of a Fractured Paradigm." *Journal of Communication* 43(4): 51–58.

Fisher, L., and B. McBride. 2016. "'Ghostbusters' Star Leslie Jones Quits Twitter After Online Harassment." *ABC News*, July 20. https://abcnews.go.com/Entertainment/ ghostbusters-star-leslie-jones-quits-twitter-online-harassment/story?id=40698459

Fox19 Digital Staff. 2020. "Bigger than a Moment: Documenting the Outcry of Our City." *FOX19, WXIX-TV*, October 27, 2020. https://www.fox19.com/2020/10/27/ bigger-than-moment-documenting-outcry-our-city/

Freedman, D. and J. A. Obar. 2016. "Media Reform: An Overview." In *Strategies for Media Reform: International Perspectives*, edited by D. Freedman, J. A. Obar, C. Martens, and R. W. McChesney. New York: Fordham University Press.

Freelon, D., C. D. McIlwain, and M. D. Clark.. *Beyond the Hashtags: #Ferguson, #BlackLivesMatter, and the Online Struggle for Offline Justice*. Center for Media and Social Impact, School of Communication, American University, Washington, D.C. https://cmsimpact.org/resource/beyond-hashtags-ferguson-blacklivesmatter -online-struggle-offline-justice/

Fuchs, C. 2015. *Culture and Economy in the Age of Social Media*. New York, NY: Routledge.

Gallagher, R. J., A. J. Reagan, C. M. Danforth, and P. S. Dodds. 2018. "Divergent Discourse Between Protests and Counter-protests: #BlackLivesMatter and #AllLivesMatter." *PLoS ONE* 13(4): e0195644. https://doi.org/10.1371/journal .pone.0195644

Gardner, K. 2018. "Social Media: Where Voices of Hate Find A Place To Preach." The Center for Public Integrity. https://publicintegrity.org/politics/social-media -where-voices-of-hate-find-a-place-to-preach/

Gersten, P. B., D. R. Grant, and C. Chiang. 2003. "Hate Online: A Content Analysis of Extremist Internet Sites." *Analyses of Social Issues and Public Policy* 3(1): 29–44.

Goffman, E. 1974. *Frame Analysis: An Essay on the Organization of Experience*. New York, NY: Harper & Row.

Goldstein, A. 2014. "Palestinian and Ferguson Protestors Link Arms Via Social Media." *Yes! Magazine*, August 15. http://www.yesmagazine.org/peace-justice/palestinians -and-ferguson-protesters-link-arms-via-social-media

Gramsci, A. 1992. *Prison Notebooks*. Edited and translated by J. A. Buttigieg. New York, NY: Columbia University Press, 1992.

Guynn, J. 2019. "Facebook While Black: Users Call It Getting 'Zucked,' Say Talking about Racism Is Censored as Hate Speech." *USA Today*, April 24. https://www

.usatoday.com/story/news/2019/04/24/facebook-while-black-zucked-users-say
-they-get-blocked-racism-discussion/2859593002/

Guynn, J. 2021. "Twitter Suspends 70,000 QAnon Accounts in Massive Purge after
Deadly Capitol Siege, Trump Ban." *USA Today*, January 11. https://www.usatoday
.com/story/tech/2021/01/11/twitter-purge-qanon-accounts-permanent-sus
pension-trump-capitol-riots/6633629002/

Haimowitz, I. 2020. "No One is Immune: The Spread of QAnon Through Social Media
and the Pandemic." Center for Strategic and International Studies. https://www
.csis.org/blogs/technology-policy-blog/no-one-immune-spread-q-anon-through
-social-media-and-pandemic

Harlow, S. 2012. "Social Media and Social Movements: Facebook and an Online
Guatemalan Justice Movement that Moved Offline." *New Media & Society* 14(2):
225–43.

Head, A. J., J. Wihbey, P. T. Metaxas, M. MacMillan, and D. Cohen. 2018. *How Students
Engage with News: Five Takeaways for Educators, Journalists and Librarians.* Knight
Foundation, Project Information Literacy, October 16. http://www.projectinfolit
.org/uploads/2/7/5/4/27541717/newsreport.pdf

Heath, B., M. Wynn, and J. Guynn. 2018. "How a Lie about George Soros and the
Migrant Caravan Multiplied Online: USA TODAY Followed the Rapid Spread of
a Social Media Conspiracy Theory about George Soros and Migrants that Grew
from Obscurity to Political Mainstream." *USA Today*, October 31. https://www
.usatoday.com/in-depth/news/nation/2018/10/31/george-soros-and-migrant-car
avan-how-lie-multiplied-online/1824633002/

Herman, E. S. 1992. *Beyond Hypocrisy: Decoding the News in an Age of Propaganda:
Including a Doublespeak Dictionary for the 1990s.* Boston, MA: South End Press.

Herman, E. S., and N. Chomsky. 1988; 2002. *Manufacturing Consent: The Political
Economy of Mass Media* (with a new introduction by the authors, 2002 ed.). New
York, NY: Pantheon Books..

Hermida, A. 2010. "From TV to Twitter: How Ambient News Became Ambient
Journalism." *M/C Journal*, 13, No. 2. https://doi.org/10.5204/mcj.220

Hermida, A., S. C. Lewis, and R. Zamith. 2014. "Sourcing the Arab Spring: A Case
Study of Andy Carvin's Sources on Twitter during the Tunisian and Egyptian
Revolutions." *Journal of Computer-Mediated Communication* 19(3): 479–99.

Hindman, M., and V. Barash. 2018. *Disinformation, "Fake News" and Influence Campaigns
on Twitter.* The Knight Foundation. Retrieved October 8, 2018. https://kf-site
-production.s3.amazonaws.com/media_elements/files/000/000/238/original/KF
-DisinformationReport-final2.pdf

Hon, L. 2016. "Social Media Framing with the Million Hoodies Movement for Justice."
Public Relations Review 42: 9–19.

Horkheimer, M. 1974. *Eclipse of Reason*. New York, NY: Continuum.

Horton, A. 2020. "Hundreds of Counter-Protesters Confront Black Lives Matter Rally in Ohio." *The Guardian*, June 18. https://www.theguardian.com/us-news/2020/jun/18/hundreds-armed-counter-protesters-confront-black-lives-matter-event-bethel-ohio

Howard, P. N., A. Duffy, D. Freelon, M. M. Hussain, W. Mari, and M. Maziad. 2011. *Opening Closed Regimes: What Was the Role of Social Media During the Arab Spring?* Social Science Research Network (SSRN). http://ssrn.com/abstract=2595096

The Irate 8. https://www.theirate8.com

Isaac, M. and J. Nicas. 2018. "Facebook Cuts Ties with Washington Firm That Sought to Discredit Social Network's Critics." *The New York Times*, November 15. https://www.nytimes.com/2018/11/15/technology/facebook-definers-soros.html?action=click&module=Top%20Stories&pgtype=Homepage

Isaac, M. and D. Wakabayashi. 2017. "Russian Influence Reached 126 Million Through Facebook Alone." *The New York Times*, October 30. Retrieved July 28, 2018 from https://www.nytimes.com/2017/10/30/technology/facebook-google-russia.html

Jackson, I. March 30, 2018. "Black Lives Matter Cincinnati changes its name, issues scathing critique of national BLM network." *Black Youth Project*. http://blackyouthproject.com/black-lives-matter-cincinnati-changes-its-name-issues-scathing-critique-of-national-blm/.

Jackson, S. J., and B. F. Welles. 2015. "Hijacking #myNYPD: Social Media Dissent and Networked Counterpublics." *Journal of Communication* 65(6): 932–52.

Jenkins, M. 2017. Private interview conducted by Jeffrey Layne Blevins at Café DeSales in Cincinnati, OH, March 16.

Johnson, B. G. 2016. "The Heckler's Veto: Using First Amendment Theory and Jurisprudence to Understand Current Audience Reactions Against Controversial Speech." *Communication Law & Policy* 21(2): 175–220.

Kang, C., M. Rosenberg, and M. Issac. 2018. "Mark Zuckerberg Defends Facebook as Furor Over Its Tactics Grows." *The New York Times*, November 15. https://www.nytimes.com/2018/11/15/technology/zuckerberg-facebook-sandberg-tactics.html

Keller, M. H. 2018. "The Business of Serving Up YouTube Views." *The New York Times*, August 12, 1: 18.

Kellner, D. 2001. *Grand Theft 2000: Media Spectacle and a Stolen Election*. New York, NY: Rowman & Littlefield.

Kilgo, D. K., R. R. Mourao, and G. Sylvie. 2018. "Martin to Brown: How Time and Platform Impact Coverage of the Black Lives Matter Movement." *Journalism Practice*. https://doi.org/10.1080/17512786.2018.1507680

Kreiss, D. 2016. "Seizing the Moment: The Presidential Campaigns' Use of Twitter During the 2012 Electoral Cycle." *New Media & Society* 18(8): 1473–90.

Lasorsa, D. L., S. C. Lewis, and A. E. Holton. 2012. "Normalizing Twitter: Journalism Practice in an Emerging Communication Space." *Journalism Studies* 13: 19–36.

Laswell, H. 1927; 1938. *Propaganda Technique in the World War* (reprint). New York, NY: Peter Smith.

Li, M., N. Turki, C. R. Izaguirre, C. DeMahy, B. L. Thibodeaux, T. Gage. 2020. "Twitter as a Tool for Social Movement: An Analysis of Feminist Activism on Social Media Communities." *Journal of Community Psychology.* https://doi.org/10.1002/jcop .22324

Liao, S. 2019. "'#IAmGay# What About You?': Storytelling, Discursive Politics, and the Affective Dimension of Social Media Activist against Censorship in China." *International Journal of Communication* 13: 2314–33.

Linvill, D. L., and P. L. Warren. 2018. "Troll Factories: The Internet Research Agency and State-Sponsored Agenda Building." Working paper. http://pwarren.people .clemson.edu/Linvill_Warren_TrollFactory.pdf

Lippmann, W. 1921; 1932. *Public Opinion* (reprint). London, England: Allen & Unwin.

Liu, W., A. Sidhu, A. M. Beacom and T. W. Valente. 2017. "Social Network Theory." In *The International Encyclopedia of Media Effects*, edited by P. Rossler, C. A. Hoffner and L. van Zoonen, 1–12. Hoboken, NJ: John Wiley & Sons, Inc.

Madhani, A. and J. Colvin. 2021. "Farewell, @realDonaldTrump: Looking back at the Twitter account's provocative history." *USA Today*, January 9. https://amp.usatoday .com/amp/6607069002?__twitter_impression=true

Mahone, J. and P. Napoli. 2020. "Hundreds of Hyperpartisan Sites are Masquerading as Local News. This Map Shows If There's One Near You." *Nieman Lab*, July 13. https://www.niemanlab.org/2020/07/hundreds-of-hyperpartisan-sites-are -masquerading-as-local-news-this-map-shows-if-theres-one-near-you/

Mandaro, L. 2014. "300 Ferguson Tweets: A Day's Work for Antonio French." *USA Today*, August 25. https://www.usatoday.com/story/news/nation-now/2014/08/25/ antonio-french-twitter-ferguson/14457633/

Manuel, S. 2020. "Ga. Protests Lead to Arrests of Vigilantes in Arbery Killing." *The Militant* 84(22), June 8. https://themilitant.com/2020/05/30/ga-protests-lead-to -arrests-of-vigilantes-in-arbery-killing/

Marcus, G. and E. Davis. 2018. "A.I. Won't Fix Fake News." *The New York Times*, October 21, SR 6.

Martinez, P. 2020. "Louisville Police Chief Fired after Fatal Shooting of Black Business Owner." *CBS News*, June 7. https://www.cbsnews.com/news/steve-conrad-louis ville-police-chief-fired-protest-shooting-death/

Marx, K. 1970. *A Contribution to the Critique of Political Economy*. Moscow: Progress Publishers.

McChesney, R. W. 1996. "The Internet and U.S. Communication Policy-Making in Historical and Critical Perspective." *Journal of Communication* 46(1): 98–124.

———. 2008. *The Political Economy of Media: Enduring Issues, Emerging Dilemmas*. New York, NY: Monthly Review Press.

McCombs, M. E., and D. L. Shaw. 1972. "The Agenda-Setting Function of Mass Media." *Public Opinion Quarterly* 36(2): 176–87.

McCormack, D. 2014. "St. Louis Rams Players Stage 'Hands Up, Don't Shoot' Protest at NFL Game in Solidarity with Ferguson Protestors." *Daily Mail* (United Kingdom), November 30. http://www.dailymail.co.uk/news/article-2855253/Five -St-Louis-Rams-players-field-arms-raised-hands-don-t-shot-gesture-solidarity -Ferguson-protesters.html

McEvoy, J. 2021. "Jury Acquits Iowa Reporter Arrested While Covering Black Lives Matter Protest." *Forbes*, March 10. https://www.forbes.com/sites/jemima mcevoy/2021/03/10/jury-acquits-iowa-reporter-arrested-while-covering-black -lives-matter-protests/?sh=6b6778664ef4

McIntyre, L. 2018. *Post-Truth*. Cambridge, MA: MIT Press.

McLaughlin, E. C., J. Berlinger, A. Fantz, and S. Almasy. 2016. "Disney Gator Attack: 2-Year-Old Boy Found Dead." *CNN*, June 16. https://www.cnn.com/2016/06/15/ us/alligator-attacks-child-disney-florida/index.html

McPhate, M. 2016. "Gorilla Killed After Child Enters Enclosure at Cincinnati Zoo." *The New York Times*, May 20. https://www.nytimes.com/2016/05/30/us/gorilla -killed-after-child-enters-enclosure-at-cincinnati-zoo.html

Meehan, E., V. Mosco, and J. Wasko. 1993. "Rethinking Political Economy: Change and Continuity." *Journal of Communication* 43(4): 105–16.

Mitchell, A., J. Gottfried, G. Stocking, M. Walker, and S. Feldi. 2019. "Many Americans Say Made-Up News Is a Critical Problem That Needs to Be Fixed." Pew Research Center, June 5. https://www.journalism.org/2019/06/05/many-americans-say -made-up-news-is-a-critical-problem-that-needs-to-be-fixed/

Mosco, V. 2009. *The Political Economy of Communication*, 2nd ed. London: Sage.

Mourao, R. R., D. K. Kilgo, and G. Sylvie. 2018. "Framing Ferguson: The Interplay of Advocacy and Journalistic Frames in Local and National Newspaper Coverage of Michael Brown." *Journalism*. https://doi.org/10.1177/1464884918778722

Moyers, B. 2007. "Life on the Plantation." Transcript of address to the Media Reform Conference, Memphis, TN, January 12. http://billmoyers.com/2007/01/12/life-on -the-plantation-january-12-2007/

Nahoon, K. and J. Hemsley. 2016. *Going Viral*. Cambridge: Polity.

Napoli, P. M. 2010. *Audience Evolution: New Technologies and Transformation of Media Audiences*. New York, NY: Columbia University Press.

Naylor, B. and R. Lucas. 2021. "Wray Stresses Role of Right-Wing Extremism In Hearing About Jan. 6 Riot." *NPR*, March 2. https://www.npr.org/2021/03/02/972539274/fbi-director-wray-testifies-before-congress-for-1st-time-since-capitol-attack

Noelle-Neumann, E. 1974. "The Spiral of Silence: A Theory of Public Opinion." *Journal of Communication* 24: 43–51.

Noone, S. 2021. "Twitter Suspends 70,000 Accounts Following US Capitol Riots." *News Nation*, January 11. https://www.newsnationnow.com/us-news/dc-riots/twitter-suspends-70000-accounts-following-riot/

Nunziato, D. 2009. *Virtual Freedom: Net Neutralitiy and Free Speech in the Internet Age*. Stanford, CA: Stanford University Press.

O'Brien, P. C. 2014. "Social Media History and Use." In *Social Media*, edited by K. Langmia, T. C. M. Tyree, P. O'Brien, and I. Sturgis. New York, NY: University Press of America.

Olteanu, A., I. Weber, and D. Gatica-Perez. 2015. "Characterizing the Demographics Behind the #BlackLivesMatter Movement." arXiv:1512.05671.

O'Malley, B. 2014. "Antonio French's Tweets Chronicled Ferguson Protests." *St. Louis Post-Dispatch*. St. Louis, MO, August 29. https://www.stltoday.com/news/multi-media/special/antonio-frenchs-tweets-chronicled-ferguson-protests/article_ffab-dcfo–405c-5ce3–82bb-e32560915ed4.html

Orwell, G. 1949. *1984*. London: Secker & Warburg.

O'Sullivan, D. 2018. "The Biggest Black Lives Matter Page on Facebook Is Fake." CNN Business, April 9. Retrieved February 10, 2019. http://money.cnn.com/2018/04/09/technology/fake-black-lives-matter-facebook-page/index.html

Owens, D. M. 2021. "#SayHerName: Breonna Taylor and Hundreds of Black Women Have Died at the Hands of Police. The Movement to Say Their Names Is Growing." *USA Today*, March 11. https://www.usatoday.com/in-depth/news/investigations/2021/03/11/sayhername-movement-black-women-police-violence/6921197002/

Papacharissi, Z. 2015. "Affective Publics and Structures of Storytelling: Sentiment, Events and Mediality." *Information, Communication & Society* 19: 307–24.

Peters, J. 2016. "More Than 20 Months after Ferguson, Ryan Reilly and Wesley Lowery Are Still Facing Charges in St. Louis County." *Columbia Journalism Review*, April 19. https://www.cjr.org/united_states_project/ryan_reilly_wesley_lowery_ferguson_charges.php

Popkan, B. 2018. "Twitter Deleted 200,000 Russian Troll Tweets. Read Them Here." NBC News, February 14, 2018. https://www.nbcnews.com/tech/social-media/now-available-more-200–000-deleted-russian-troll-tweets-n844731

Rainie, L. and B. Wellman. 2012. *Networked: The New Social Operating System.* Cambridge, MA: MIT Press.

Roberts, D. 2017. "America Is Facing an Epistemic Crisis." *Vox*, November 2. https://www.vox.com/policy-and-politics/2017/11/2/16588964/america-epistemic-crisis

Robinson, S. 2011. "'Journalism as Process': The Organizational Implications of Participatory Online News." *Journalism & Communication Monographs* 13(3): 137–210.

Roeder, O. 2018. "Why We're Sharing 3 Million Russian Troll Tweets." FiveThirtyEight, July 31, 2018. https://fivethirtyeight.com/features/why-were-sharing-3-million-russian-troll-tweets/

Rossman, S., M. Wynn, J. Guynn, and B. Heath. "How a few shady social media posts fed a viral firestorm over Covington Catholic (and why it will happen again)." USA Today, Feb. 19, 2019. https://www.usatoday.com/story/news/investigations/2019/02/19/covington-catholic-outrage-spread-shady-facebook-and-twitter-posts/2667213002/

Russomanno, J. 2017. "Falsehoods and Fallacies: Brandeis, Free Speech and Trumpism." *Communication Law & Policy* 22(3): 155–87.

Shedden, D. 2015. "Today in Media History: 2009 Hudson River Crash-Landing Photo Sent with Twitter." Poynter, January 15. https://www.poynter.org/reporting-editing/2015/today-in-media-history-2009-hudson-river-crash-landing-photo-sent-with-twitter/

Shiller, R. J. 2019. *Narrative Economics.* Princeton, NJ: Princeton University Press.

Shirky, C. 2008. *Here Comes Everybody: The Power of Organizing Without Organizations.* New York, NY: The Penguin Press.

Silverman, C. 2016. "This Analysis Shows How Viral Fake Election News Stories Outperformed Real News on Facebook." *Buzzfeed*, November 16. https://www.buzzfeednews.com/article/craigsilverman/viral-fake-election-news-outperformed-real-news-on-facebook

Silverman, C. and L. Alexander. 2016. "How Teens In The Balkans Are Duping Trump Supporters With Fake News." *Buzzfeed*, November 3. https://www.buzzfeednews.com/article/craigsilverman/how-macedonia-became-a-global-hub-for-pro-trump-misinfo

Southern Poverty Law Center. 2020. "Methodology: How Hate Groups Are Identified and Categorized." March 18. https://www.splcenter.org/news/2020/03/18/methodology-how-hate-groups-are-identified-and-categorized

Stanglin, D. 2018. "Trump, via Twitter, Says Social Media Discriminates Against GOP, Conservative Voices." *USA Today*, August 18. https://www.usatoday.com/story/news/2018/08/18/trump-says-social-media-discriminates-against-gop-con servatives/1030478002/

Stewart, A. J., M. Mosleh, M. Diakonova, A. A. Arechar, D. G. Rand, and J. B. Plotkin. 2019. "Information Gerrymandering and Undemocratic Decisions." *Nature* 573: 117–21.

Stewart, D. R. and J. Littau. 2016. "Up, Periscope: Mobile Streaming Video Technologies, Privacy in Public, and the Right to Record." *Journalism & Mass Communication Quarterly* 93(2): 312–31.

Timber, C. 2019. "The Strange Birth, Death and Rebirth of Russian Troll Account 'AllForUSA.'" *The Washington Post*, August 7, A4.

Tornoe, R. 2017. "Two Popular Conservative Twitter Personalities Were Just Outed as Russian Trolls: Jenna Abrams and Pamela Moore Were Followed by Tens of Thousands, Including Members of Trump's Campaign." *The Philadelphia Inquirer*, November 3. http://www.philly.com/philly/news/politics/presidential/russia-fake -twitter-facebook-posts-accounts-trump-election-jenna-abrams-20171103.html

Tucker, R. C. 1978. *The Marx-Engels Reader*, 2nd ed. New York, NY: W. W. Norton & Company.

Tufekci, Z. 2017. *Twitter and Tear Gas: The Power and Fragility of Networked Protest.* New Haven, CT: Yale University Press.

U.S. House of Representatives, Permanent Select Committee on Intelligence Social Media, 2017. Retrieved February 10, 2019. https://democrats-intelligence.house .gov/facebook-ads/social-media-advertisements.htm

Usher, N. 2016. "The Appropriation/Amplification Model of Citizen Journalism." *Journalism Practice*, 2016. http://dx.doi.org/10.1080/17512786.2016.1223552

Wang, R., W. Liu, and S. Gao. 2016. "Hashtags and Information Virality in Networked Social Movement." *Online Information Review* 40(7): 850–66.

Wang, S. 2017. "Twitter Sidestepped Russian Account Warnings, Former Worker Says." *Bloomberg*, November 3. https://www.bloomberg.com/news/articles/2017–11-03/ former-twitter-employee-says-fake-russian-accounts-were-not-taken-seriously

Ward, C., K. Polglase, S. Shukla, G. Mezzofiore, and T. Lister. 2020. "Russian election meddling is back—via Ghana and Nigeria—and in your feeds." CNN, April 11. https://www.cnn.com/2020/03/12/world/russia-ghana-troll-farms-2020-ward/ index.html

Wineburg, S., S. McGrew, J. Breakstone, and T. Ortega. 2016. *Evaluating Information: The Cornerstone of Civic Online Reasoning.* Stanford Digital Repository. https://purl .stanford.edu/fv751yt5934

Wojcik, S., S. Messing, A. Smith, L. Rainie, and P. Hitlin. 2018. "Bots in the Twittersphere: An Estimated Two-Thirds of Tweeted Links to Popular Websites Are Posted by Automated Accounts—Not Human Beings." Pew Research Center, April 9. Retrieved February 10, 2019. http://www.pewinternet.org/2018/04/09/bots-in-the-twittersphere/

"Woman streams graphic video of boyfriend shot by police." CNN, July 7, 2016. http://www.cnn.com/videos/us/2016/07/07/graphic-video-minnesota-police-shooting-philando-castile-ryan-young-pkg-nd.cnn/video/playlists/philando-castile-shot-in-minnesota/.

Woolley, S. C. and D. Guilbeault. 2017. "Computational Propaganda in the United States of America: Manufacturing Consensus Online." In *Project on Computational Propaganda*, edited by S. Woolley and P. N. Howard. Oxford Internet Institute, Oxford, UK. http://comprop.oii.ox.ac.uk/publishing/working-papers/computational-propaganda-in-the-united-states-of-america-manufacturing-consensus-online/

Wortham, Jenna. 2016. "Black Tweets Matter: 'BlackTwitter' Has Become a Powerful Force for Political Activism, Lightning-Fast Cultural Commentary-and a Place to Just Hang Out." *Smithsonian Magazine*, September 2016. http://www.smithsonianmag.com/arts-culture/black-tweets-matter-180960117/

Zadrozny, B. and B. Collins. 2020. "Videos, Threats, but Few Signs Protests Have Been Stoked by 'Outsider' Extremist Groups." *NBC News*, May 31. https://www.nbcnews.com/tech/security/videos-threats-few-signs-protests-have-been-stoked-outsider-extremist-n1220451

Zimmerman, K. A. and J. Empsak. 2017. "Internet History Timeline: ARPANET to the World Wide Web." *Live Science*, June 27. https://www.livescience.com/20727-internet-history.html

About the authors

Jeffrey Layne Blevins is a professor in the Journalism Department at the University of Cincinnati and editor of the scholarly journal *Democratic Communiqué*. A frequent opinion-editorial columnist, Dr. Blevins's commentary on media policy and ethics has appeared in *USA Today*, *Cincinnati Enquirer*, *St. Louis Post-Dispatch* and other venues. In 2009 he served as a federal grant reviewer for the Broadband Technology Opportunities Program administered by the National Telecommunications and Information Administration and the U.S. Department of Commerce.

James Jaehoon Lee is Associate Professor of Digital Humanities, Director of the Digital Scholarship Center, and Associate Vice Provost for Digital Scholarship at the University of Cincinnati.